Addicted and Convicted:

Letters from a Lost Daughter

Addicted and Convicted:
Letters from a Lost Daughter

by Elizabeth Elliot
with her mother Sheila Ellin

Bridgeton, New Jersey
2023

ISBN: 9798857062470

Library of Congress Control Number: 2023915464

Imprint: Independently published

First edition 2023

Bridgeton, New Jersey

Elizabeth's last name, several other names, and several identifying details have been changed to protect the privacy of some members of her family.

Table of Contents

Introduction

All About Me – Written by Elizabeth in 8th Grade, 1999

My name is Elizabeth. I am 14 and in eighth grade. Right now my hobbies include lacrosse, dancing, and playing the clarinet. I really like listening to music and reading. My favorite foods are filet mignon, mashed potatoes, and candy. The two most important things in my life are my family and my friends.

It was December when my mother received an early Christmas present – me. From age 3 to age 5, I attended nursery school, where my mom worked at the time. When I was four years old, my parents divorced. Just before I went to kindergarten, my mom and I moved across the street from my grandparents. My favorite part of my kindergarten year was when we went to _____ to let the baby turtles go. It was very special because we were the class that started that tradition. Now I'm in eighth grade and I love it because it's the oldest class in the school. I can't wait until high school!

Next year I would like to go to a Christian high school because I do not want to go to a big high school, but I will probably end up going to the local public high school. I hope to be on the track team if I could overcome my laziness or I may be in the band. College is a place I plan to go to. I do not know where I want to go but I know that it won't be nearby. I'm going to keep my options open, so hopefully some college will spark my interest.

After college I want to find a career that I like that pays well. I picture myself living in either London, England or in New York City. I would like to get married in my early twenties and have children about two years after that. I hope to marry an attractive, tall, strong, kind, smart, and funny guy. I would like to have two sets of twins – and the

1

first will be one girl and one boy, and the second would be the same. I can't wait to have a happy life with loving family and friends, good health, and lots of money.

Elizabeth's Diary 6th Grade through 8th Grade

August 25, 1996: Elizabeth's Private Diary, Age 11

There is this boy that goes to my beach. He is so hot. His name is Steve Miller. The reason I know it is because he got an award at the basketball awards and they announced it. He is great looking!

October 27, 1996: Elizabeth's Private Diary, Age 11

Yesterday I went to this thing at the firehouse and it was so fun. We went on a jumpy thing and hit each other with inflatable balls. After we left the firehouse, we went into town. We went to a pay phone and called 1-800-5-France.They said stuff in French, and Tommy said that "Volevu cushe avec moi" means "Will you sleep with me tonight?" It was so funny.

November 29, 1996: Elizabeth's Private Diary, Age 11

Last Friday, there was a dance. I danced with this "yuck" guy 3 times. Everybody in the sixth grade (girls) is dating except me and Lauren SB. I am so jealous!!!! I will never be able to date because I am taller than everyone in my class and I am not pretty at all!

January 20, 1997: Elizabeth's Private Diary, Age 12

I have no idea what to write. I guess I'll think of something. I have it! I don't know why, but I just feel so empty but nothing in my life is going wrong; I wish I didn't have to go to school. I'd just have fun and live freely. I love my family but I wish they wouldn't embarrass me.

July 23, 1997: Elizabeth's Private Diary, Age 12

The guy across the street is so hot! It's not fair that I'm not pretty! I wish I could go out w/ him. I wish I could at least go out w/ someone. Most of the reason why I'm not pretty is my freckles and the wrinkles under my eyes. Too bad! Bye!

May 17, 1998: Elizabeth's Private Diary, Age 13

I really wish I was going out with someone right now. I also want a better house. I know it's so superficial and shallow, but I'm embarrassed of it. When I'm older I want to be rich, get my belly-button pierced, get a tattoo, and try smoking. I hate school. I wish it was outlawed.

May 18, 1998: Elizabeth's Private Diary, Age 13

Sometimes I get so pissed at my mom and dad for saying mean things about each other. I also get mad at [stepmom] for telling my dad the things I do wrong.: I wish my mom would let me get my belly-button pierced. The only reason she will not let me is because it takes about a year to heal. I might ask my dad if he will let me get it pierced and if he says he will let me, (which I am almost positive that he won't) I could move into the house with him and [stepmom]. My mom says I would not even last a week living with him because of all the junk I eat over here and how healthy they eat over there. I actually think that she just might be right!

August 16, 1998: Elizabeth's Private Diary, Age 13

My stepmom's dog got hit by a car and died. I still can't believe it. I feel so bad for [stepmom]. I miss him.

August 31, 1998: Elizabeth's Private Diary, Age 13

I am so bored! There is nothing to do in this stupid town. My mom won't let me watch television, everybody on my street has left town. Even if I do hang out with Lauren the only thing to do is go to the beach and I can't do that all day or I'll have skin cancer by the time I'm 18. Lauren, [stepmom], Mom, and I are going to Yo! Philadelpia [music/food festival] on Labor Day.

September 8, 1998: Elizabeth's Private Diary, Age 13

Today I hung out w/ KC, Lauren, & Lisa. We went on the internet and talked to some 18 year old guy. We also talked to Zack but he was a little drunk. We saw Brian & Tommy down town. It was funny because we were all awkward. We couldn't think of anything to talk about. I want to meet Zack. Tommy bleached his hair. It looks weird.

September 18, 1998: Elizabeth's Private Diary, Age 13

I sorta kinda like Brian. Tommy has gotten a little hot. When we went to Yo! Philly, Mr. Greengenes played and one guy (Johnny Phat) was the HOTTEST person I have ever seen in my whole life. I can't wait for the dance next week because it's boring around here. I am going to a swing-dancing workshop. I can't wait!

September 23, 1998: Elizabeth's Private Diary, Age 13

I can't believe I actually have a picture of him. (Johnny Phat) Here is a list of guys who I'd love to make out with: 5) the blonde guy from the wedding I worked w/ [stepmom] 4) Joshua Jackson from Dawson's Creek: 3) Christian: 2) Drew: 1) Johnny Phat. I hope Mr. Greengenes is still playing when I am allowed to go to bars. They can actually play pretty damn good as well as having a hotter than hot guy in the band.

November 9, 1998: Elizabeth's Private Diary, Age 13

I forgot to write about this in July, but my mom and I went to the birthday party of my mom's co-worker's grandson, Michael P. He is 15, is kinda short, cute, and goes to a Christian high school. He is also sweet. It was a pool party and we were playing Marco Polo and he told me to speak up because I had a pretty voice. Then we got really close because he cornered me when he was 'it'. He is like the perfect guy except for the fact that he's short and older. I wonder if it's possible to fall in love with somebody when you've only met them once? I actually think so. I really wish that I could get to see him again. Brian beat up Morgan but didn't get in trouble because Morgan pretended he tripped as an excuse.

December 5, 1998: Elizabeth's Private Diary, Age 13

I HATE my mom's boyfriend, Ed. He is bald, has a mustache, and is a washed out old surfer. I didn't feel like watching a movie with them so I stayed in my room. I went out there to ask my mom a question and he had his FUCKING arm around her. My mother should start acting her own age and start leaving the dating shit to me.:

December 6, 1998: Elizabeth's Private Diary, Age 13

Lauren and I have decided that I will go out with and marry her cousin, Greg. He's cute, funny, nice, and I already liked him. Lauren is going to try to fix me up with him this summer. Over Christmas break, we might try to go to the mall and stay at his house. I can't wait until the summer.

January 20, 1999: Elizabeth's Private Diary, Age 14

On December 27, my mom, Ed (I HATE HIM), and I went to Michael P's house. I really like him. Whenever he talked to me, he always found some way to touch me. My mom told his grandmother that I had a crush on him and she said he might have a crush on me.

February 6, 1999: Elizabeth's Private Diary, Age 14

I ♥ Michael P! He's hot, sweet, funny, and all this other great stuff. His grandmother and my mom think he likes me too! I sure as hell hope so! I can't wait until I see him again.

February 12, 1999: Elizabeth's Private Diary, Age 14

My mom is on the phone with Ed & I think they're breaking up! <u>YESSSS!!!</u>
I hope they do!

April 7, 1999: Elizabeth's Private Diary, Age 14

I hate my father; but I still love him. He sure knows just the right words to use when putting me down that will make me cry. He's called me spoiled, selfish, and ungrateful, but if he had to spend one hour being at my one friend's house, he'd know that I'm far from that. I am about the most well-behaved child that I know. I wasn't eating my dinner fast enough – I have to chew for God's sake. I don't think he even has a conscience – he never apologizes for his behavior.

My 8th grade classmates made this for me!

Enjoys Seventh Heaven
Loves the Beach
Is a Good Friend
Zodiac Sign is Capricorn
Awesome Clarinet Player
Best Speller in the School
Excellent Lacrosse Player
The Concert Mistress
Hates Mint

June 19, 1999: Elizabeth's Private Diary, Age 14

Last night was great! It was [eighth grade] graduation. Poor Brian; his voice cracked a lot during his speech. His brothers were laughing so much. My outrageously long speech (it consisted of saying hello, saluting the flag, & the Nat'l Anthem) went fine. I was shaking so much in my 3 inch heels as I walked to the stage. I was so glad I didn't have to talk that much. I think I'm really going to miss my class, the 8th grade class of 1999.

High School

High School (September 1999 to June 2003)

Elizabeth did well academically in high school and was active in band, lacrosse, and dance. Her most memorable high school experience was an exchange trip to England in 10th grade. Elizabeth wrote about the experience in her College Admission Essay below:

Elizabeth's College Admission Essay – Student Exchange Trip to England

My parents divorced when I was four years old. My mother got custody of me in the divorce and I had been living with her from the age of four, until the summer of 2002 (the summer before my senior year). Visits to my father's house usually occurred once a week.

I have experienced some hard times, both economically and emotionally, and I am grateful for them. They have made me a stronger, more compassionate, and independent person. The key event in my life that made me come to the realization that I had the aforementioned qualities was the participation in a student exchange program to England. There, for the first time, I was able to put my life lessons to use and start making decisions for myself.

During my childhood, I was extremely shy and sensitive. Even going to family gatherings such as holidays and birthday parties made me very uneasy. Making the decision to participate in my high school's exchange program was a turning point in my life. In my sophomore year of high school I had the opportunity to go on a four week learning experience to England.

I worked hard during the summer to save the money I needed for my trip. I conversed with the British student, Carly, who I would stay with. We grew considerably close and were both extremely excited about meeting face to face. A month before I was to arrive, Carly's father died suddenly and unexpectedly. We all decided that I would still stay with Carly, her mother, and 10 year old sister, and serve as a distraction to aid in the healing of their devastating loss.

Most of the trip took place in a small village approximately 45 miles northwest of London. Including myself, six students participated in the program. The five students I traveled with had known each other since elementary school. Not knowing any of them personally, this made it difficult for me to feel comfortable around them. Although I was afraid of being in a new situation, I had always been intrigued by England, new people, and other cultures.

The format of the exchange program was to stay at the English student's home. During the week days, the American students, our chaperone, and one of the teachers from the English school would go on day trips. These visits included Stratford-upon-Avon, London, Oxford and Leighton-Buzzard. My personal highlight of the trip was an overnight stay to the city of York. On this trip we learned many interesting facts about this history-rich city. We walked around the city wall, toured the medieval York Minster, visited many interesting shops, and went on a haunted walking tour of the downtown area.

Living with Carly and her family during such an emotional period, I utilized my skills of compassion and empathy. I was able to appreciate life and family more when viewing the effects of loss. Carly and I formed a close bond that stemmed from the commonalities in our personalities and interests. When Carly and the British students came to the United States for a month, about six months later, we had a great time. On Spring Break, my Mom, Carly, and I went to Disney World. Carly's visit was definitely a success, and I was glad I had made the decision to take part in the cultural exchange.

2002

In 2002, in the spring of Elizabeth's junior year of high school, I discovered that she had smoked marijuana. Elizabeth told me she had just been experimenting. Several years later she told me that she had smoked marijuana daily, because it helped her social anxiety – which had bothered her since early childhood.

Elizabeth spent her senior year of high school with her father, her stepmom, and her recently adopted baby stepbrother. I moved to Colorado to stay with my brother and his future wife, then I settled in Moab, Utah. Liz and my parents came out west to visit in the summer. Elizabeth then came with her cousin to visit me, my brother Jim, and his future wife Debbie in Colorado at Christmas. I came back to New Jersey in the spring for three months for my brother's wedding, Elizabeth's prom, her final dance recital, and her high school graduation in June. When apart, Elizabeth and I talked on the phone, emailed, and wrote letters.

September 13, 2002: Email from her Dad's house in NJ to me in Colorado

hey mommy,what's new?
how do you like being 40? at least you're not as old as [friend]
i signed up for the November SAT's

we are doing the dumbest dance for the dance recital – it's the 25th anniversary of the show and we're dancing to jockjams megamix from like 1998– really lame – it's been done, very cliché, and our dance moves aren't even going to be original

PLEASE GET MY FREAKIN' INSTALL CD FROM MOAB – I AM GOING CRAZY BC I CAN'T BURN ANY MUSIC!!!!!!!!!!!!!!!!!!!!!!!AND SEND IT EXPRESS A.S.A. FRICKIN'P.

there's a college fair tomorrow night, so i think i'll drag laurie there

luv ya lots, call me, send me lots of pics

bye – bye my little 40 year old (JK)

elizabeth

September 30, 2002: Email from her Dad's house in NJ to me in Colorado

hey momma

i certainly do want to talk to you but i'm freakin' tired bc I have to get up at 5:30am for school

i like psych a lot, fun class, actually interesting

i haven't called bc I sorta had a large long distance bill between u and carly [English exchange student]

but i'll call this weekend

there really isn't much new which is why i don't talk a lot

i miss u too!!

thank you sooooo much for the pictures

and especially the story about fashion week!!

i'll talk to u soon mama, love, Elizabeth

November 19, 2002: Letter from her dad's house in NJ to me in Colorado

HEY MOMMY!

Here is the "Got Milk" ad that I promised. Now you have to do me a favor – think of some songs from the 70s that are cool that I can download. Por ejemple: Led Zeppelin "Dyer Maker" & Grateful Dead "Casey Jones"…ones I remember listening to w/ you when I was little on 100.7. That would be much appreciated.

Also, WHERE SHOULD I APPLY TO COLLEGE?

My life is going pretty well. Lauren's finally done w/band, and for once in my life I'm having success in the boy department. It's not as fun living here, but I can deal w/ it. I cannot wait to come visit you and Uncle Jimmy and Debbie! [cousin] & I can do some cooking while we're there. (We'll try not to poison u or anything).

I'm back to reading a book constantly. Right now it's *Middlesex,* by Jeffrey Eugenides, author of cult hit *The Virgin Suicides.* It's amazing how much money u can save by going to the library! I am thoroughly enjoying "Gilmore Girls" now that Rory and Jess are FINALLY together! But every week I only get to see the last ½ hour of it bc I have dance and am too lazy to read the directions (let alone look for them) to record on the VCR. Oh well, Laurie keeps me up to date on the beginnings. Luv u lots! Send me letters!

Love, Elizabeth

March 12, 2003: Email from her dad's house in NJ to me in Moab

hey mommy, sup? I really cannot wait until u come home.
    i miss u so much, just wanted to tell u that.
    i'm looking forward to u calling me tonight.
    i love you, elizabeth

March 16, 2003: Email from her dad's house in NJ to me in Moab

What up mommy? It's so beautiful today, sunny skies, pretty warm (55-60), I'm trying to think of something to do outside. You should know that Lauren & I are the only seniors to have a perfect attendance record for lacrosse. I cannot wait for spring break, although I have yet to think of anything fun and affordable to do. So start brainstorming for me. Did I tell you about my new Italian pen-pal? Well today I'm going to write back to her. I hope you're having a great day! I miss you! I love you! Elizabeth

June 2003, High School Graduation Age 18

Elizabeth got 1400 out of 1600 on her SAT s and was offered scholarships to two colleges.

College, First Rehab and Beyond

August 2003 to December 2003 Age 18 (College)

Elizabeth decided to attend _____ to major in Apparel Design and Fashion Merchandising. When she got to college, Elizabeth experienced social anxiety and depression. She did not attend classes and so she flunked out of college.

February 2004: Email from Liz in NJ to me in Moab

yo mom
what up
i'm doing ok
hope you are very happy
and taking walks
in the sun
i miss you too
have a nice day
love, Elizabeth

Moab

Elizabeth came out to Moab for a visit and we took a road trip around the Four Corners area. Elizabeth met with a therapist a few times, who advised her to continue with a therapist when she went back to New Jersey the next week.

March 2004 to July 2004 New Jersey

Back in New Jersey, Elizabeth got a job as a waitress at a local golf and country club.

Elizabeth worked at the country club for 5 months. The chef there and his friends introduced her to cocaine.

Elizabeth lived with my parents for a while, and a psychologist friend of theirs saw her as a courtesy. The psychologist told Elizabeth she was depressed and should be on medication. Unfortunately, just a few days later, the chef and friends where she worked introduced her to heroin. A few months later, Elizabeth called me in Moab, crying. She said she had something terrible to tell me – she was addicted to heroin. We got her into a 30-day rehab in South Florida.

August 1 to September 1, 2004, Age 19: Behavioral Health of the Palm Beaches Rehab

Elizabeth adjusted quickly to rehab. She was diagnosed with depression and an eating disorder. The rehab did not put her on medication because their policy was no psych medication until after six months of abstinence.

I went down for Parent's Weekend and met Elizabeth's roommate Cheryl and her boyfriend Matt.

Elizabeth told me she believed she had to stop using heroin and cocaine, but she believed she could still smoke weed.

In September 2004, Elizabeth and Cheryl got out of rehab and moved in together in Lake Worth, Florida. Things seemed to go well until Cheryl's boyfriend sent her heroin through the mail. Elizabeth smoked it and Cheryl shot up and overdosed. Elizabeth called 911 and Cheryl was okay. Cheryl's father sent her to a long-term rehab. Elizabeth moved in with Matt.

16

Everything was fine until Matt had to drive a friend to
New Jersey. Elizabeth ended up flying back to New Jersey.
There was some missed communication. Elizabeth and
Matt lost contact. Matt went back to Florida, Elizabeth
stayed in New Jersey. A poem and a journal entry Elizabeth
wrote, but never gave to Matt, follows.

Matt

I was your princess, your angel
with eyes like the Indian Ocean
and one day we'd go to the Herradura Falls
and make love in a place just as
beautiful as you made me feel.

Matt,
When we were together, that was one of the very
few times in my life that I truly felt like everything was
going to be okay. I felt like I never wanted to be with
anyone else – no one else in the world appealed to me.
Every day was special because I spent it with you. It
was my only relationship not on drugs which means it
was the only honest one. I didn't have anything to
escape from because all I needed was you. No one
could ever make me smile the way you did. As we got
to know each other, I started to realize that there was a
reason we were supposed to meet under those
circumstances – so we would understand each other and
start new lives together. It was hard for you to accept
the things I did in the low point of my life but you did
and made me feel special every second I was with you,
or talking to you, or just thinking of you. Just staying in
and playing cards without being fucked up was more
fun than I've had with anyone else. All I pray for is that
you'll come back to me someday because I know we

were meant to be. I'll be waiting for you for the rest of my life. I love you more than anything.

November 26, 2004: New Jersey

Several months after Elizabeth lost touch with Matt, it was Thanksgiving, and she was visiting her grandparents. My aunt, uncle, cousins, and I were also visiting my parents for the holiday. Elizabeth and her cousin walked downtown to look at the shops. A few hours later, her cousin called and told us Elizabeth had been arrested and was being held at the police station.
Elizabeth was charged with:
- One count possession marijuana 1.56 grams
- One count possession CDS [controlled dangerous substance, cocaine] .171 grams
- One count shoplifting

When her family came to the police station, Elizabeth was released.

After this arrest, Elizabeth wasn't permitted to live with her dad. She moved into a cheap motel and got a waitressing job. She met Bob, who became her boyfriend. After there was a stabbing at the motel, Bob's parents let Elizabeth move into their house with them.

February 14, 2005: Elizabeth's Private Journal

How can I trust Bob when he's proved he can't be trusted? Why didn't I go back to Florida to Matt? Bob <u>lies all the fucking time</u> and doesn't see the wrong in it. He promised at the beginning if I was his girl, everything would be great and he would treat me right.

18

Elizabeth's charges

Regarding her drug charges, since Elizabeth had no juvenile charges or prior adult charges, they planned to put her into Pretrial Intervention to avoid jail or prison. Elizabeth had a Substance Abuse Evaluation in preparation for being enrolled in Pretrial Intervention.

Substance Abuse Evaluation: April 2005

Drug/Alcohol Use

Ms.___ said her first use of a substance was at the age of 15 when she tried alcohol and marijuana. She admitted to using the following substances in the past 30 days:

Alcohol – to intoxication, 6 days
Cocaine – 1 day
Cannabis – 12 days

She admitted to using the following substances on a regular basis in her lifetime:

Cannabis – 4 years

She said she has used a needle to administer drugs in the past, but does not consider herself an IV drug user. A problem with cannabis was identified by the interviewer during the assessment interview. Ms.___ reported no abstinence from her drug of choice. She said she has never had delirium tremens, and she has never overdosed on drugs. Ms.___ said she was treated for drug abuse on one occasion. According to Ms.___, she last attended 28 days of inpatient treatment eight months ago at Behavioral Health of the Palm Beaches, in Lake Worth, Florida. She said she successfully completed the treatment. She stated she was last evaluated for alcohol/drugs at Behavioral Health of the Palm Beaches.

19

Ms.___ said she has received no outpatient counseling, nor has she attended AA/NA during this time period. She reported no alcohol problems in the past 30 days; however, she reported four days of drug problems during the same time period. She says she does not see a need for alcohol treatment but sees a moderate need for drug treatment.

Ms.___ said she drinks alcohol once every three weeks, in the amount of 1 pint within a night. She said her last drink of alcohol was a week ago. Ms.___ said she has experienced blackouts from excessive drinking. She said she used heroin (IV) daily, in the amount of 3 bags a day, for one month. She said her last use of heroin was October, 2004. Ms. ___ said she has used methadone a few times, as a substitute when she could not obtain heroin. She said she smoked marijuana regularly, in the amount of 3 blunts a day. She said her last use of marijuana was 3 days ago. She said she snorted cocaine daily, for 3 months and smoked crack "a few times". She said her last use of cocaine was 3 weeks ago. Ms.___ said she has used pain pills, phenobarbital, xanax, and ecstasy. Elizabeth said she has experimented with PCP and nitrous.

Legal Status
She is awaiting charges, trial, or sentencing for Possession of CDS (cocaine). She described her legal problems as slightly serious, and said counseling or referral for these legal problems is moderately important.

Family History
Ms. ___'s mother Sheila, resides in Moab, Utah. Her father and his partner live in New Jersey. She has two sisters (half siblings) and one brother (step sibling). She explains that her parents were married but divorced when she was four years old. She remained living with her mother. At the age of 17, she went to live with her father

20

and his partner, but is presently prohibited from their residence due to her drug use. She states she has contact with her father but the relationship is strained. She has a good relationship with her mother and speaks to her frequently. Ms.___ is residing with her boyfriend and his family. She plans to remain there while in Pretrial Intervention.

Elizabeth said the following members on her mother's side of the family have had significant problems with: mother – psychiatric

She reported the following members on her father's side of the family have had significant problems with: uncle – alcohol

Family/Social Relationships
Ms. _____ reported two close friends, and said she had close, reciprocal relationships with her: mother, sexual partner, friends.

She said she spends most of her free time with friends and is satisfied with spending free time this way. According to Ms. ____, she has experienced serious problems in the past 30 days with her: father.

She reported that during her lifetime she has experienced serious problems getting along with her: father.

Ms. ____ reported no abuse in the past 30 days. She said that during her lifetime she has been abused: sexually, but does not know who or chooses not to identify the person.

Elizabeth indicated that treatment or counseling would be considerably important for her family problems and would not be important for her social problems.

21

Psychiatric Status

Ms.___ said she has been treated as a private patient or on an outpatient basis for psychological problems on three occasions. She reported having experienced the following psychological problems during the past 30 days: serious depression, serious anxiety or tension, trouble controlling violent behavior.

She said she has not experienced any serious thoughts of suicide in the past 30 days and has not attempted suicide during this time period.

Ms.___ reported having experienced the following psychological problems during her lifetime: serious depression, serious anxiety or tension, serious thoughts of suicide.

Ms.___ said she was initially diagnosed with Depression in June, 2004. She said she is not taking any medications for Depression at this time.

Interviewer's Assessment

Ms.___ was pleasant and cooperative at the time of her interview. She abuses marijuana. She has been dependent on heroin. At the time of her offense, she alleged that she was under the influence of marijuana. Despite her most recent charge, she continues to use drugs. Ms.___ stated that she suffers from depression. She appeared to self-medicate with illicit drugs to eliminate anxiety and depression. Ms.___ doesn't have an extensive history of alcohol & drug use, however, she has abused several different types of drugs within a 1-2 year period. She had prior short term residential alcohol/drug treatment within this year, but she did not follow the Aftercare Recommendations as specified. She would benefit from

Intensive Outpatient D/A Treatment, AA/NA Meetings, Random Drug Monitoring, and a Mental Health Assessment.

Drug Screen Results
Positive for marijuana and benzodiazepines.

On May 5, 2005, Elizabeth was enrolled in Pretrial Intervention for 18 months.

The requirements were:
- IOP (Intensive Outpatient)
- Random Drug Tests
- AA/NA
- Mental Health Assessment

July 13, 2005: Sheila's Journal

Today I called Elizabeth, she hadn't been calling because she was very depressed, she cried on the phone about Matt [soul mate] in Florida. I agreed to help her find info on him. All I could find out was that Matt hadn't died in Florida and that he had no criminal record nationwide.

Then Liz cried and told me she had met her cousin Grant, living on the streets, and he was addicted to crack. She hadn't seen him since she was a little kid. Grant was born deaf. Grant's father ____, (Elizabeth's father's brother), died when Grant was only 5 years old. So Grant has had a rough life. And Elizabeth was so sad about it. Her 32 year old cousin being addicted to crack and living on the streets had really got her down.

July 14, 2005: New Jersey

Elizabeth's boyfriend Bob was pulled over for going 70 mph in a 50-mph zone. Bob got tickets for speeding and driving on a suspended license. The cop ran Elizabeth's license and a warrant for her arrest came up for not appearing in court on a traffic ticket. The cop searched her bag and found weed and cocaine paraphernalia.

Elizabeth was charged with:

- Possession of marijuana
- Possession of cocaine
- Possession of paraphernalia

Elizabeth was taken to jail. Bob and Elizabeth's pop-pop, my dad, went to bail her out.

August 17, 2005: New Jersey

Elizabeth's boyfriend Bob was arrested on August 17, 2005, and Elizabeth was released on her own recognizance, with a charge of "hindering the apprehension of a fugitive" remaining open for one year. She was released so that she could make her Pretrial Intervention appointment. At the appointment, Elizabeth was found eligible for detox and residential placement.

August 18, 2005: Pretrial Intervention Status Hearing

Elizabeth's probation officer told the judge that she had not been following the Pretrial Intervention requirements. In addition, Elizabeth tested positive for cocaine before the hearing, which was a violation of Pretrial Intervention. The judge ordered her locked up in county jail until a long-term bed in rehab became available…they took Elizabeth away in handcuffs, crying.

Jail and Second Rehab

September 23, 2005: Letter from County Jail

Hi Mommy!

I just went to court [from jail] yesterday. I left at 9am and didn't get back until 4pm! I sat in a cell and read *Mystic River* until I finally saw [lawyer] at 2pm. He basically said I needed to plead guilty to one of my new charges…the other new one would be dropped and they would keep me on PTI [Pretrial Intervention] on the condition that I complete Straight & Narrow [locked rehab]. I'm getting two extra years PTI & I have to pay $1100 more in fines in addition to the $1300 approx. that I owe. Then an hour later I went before Judge A (aaaagh!) and she asked me all these questions pertaining to whether or not I understood that I didn't have to plead guilty.

It kinda freaked me out & made me second guess my decision. Because I never got to read my discovery & I wasn't even indicted for the crime I pled guilty to – it could have been thrown out! But at this point I just want to get out of jail. This deal was to avoid drug court which I know I could not handle so hopefully I did the right thing. What do you think? If I leave Straight & Narrow, there will be an immediate bench warrant issued.

I can't wait to be able to talk to you. I just feel so much pain & shame that I don't like anyone getting in my head, so I just shut everyone out. There has never been a time when I haven't felt bad about how I treat you, that I haven't been grateful to God for blessing me with the most understanding, intelligent, caring & loving mother. I need to stop taking you for granted because life is fragile and I don't want to hurt you. Even though I don't show it, I've always understood how lucky I am to have you. I thank you for everything you've taught me, for the traits, good and bad, you've given me, and for your ability to make me appreciate so many different things. My best trait I got from you, it's still there, that's empathy, but I've seen such horrible things in the past few years I feel jaded and callous. I want to change. I'm still the same person. I'm sorry for everything. I want you to be proud.

I love you forever Mom, Love, Little Lizzie

September 26, 2005: Sent to Straight & Narrow Court Ordered Locked Rehab

Elizabeth was taken from county jail to Straight & Narrow, a court ordered locked rehab in Secaucus, New Jersey. She was told Pretrial Intervention required her to stay there six months. She was put on medications for her depression and anxiety.

October 4, 2005: Letter from Straight & Narrow Court Ordered Rehab

Hi Mommy,

I miss you. I'm sorry I've been such a brat and a disappointment. I don't want to let you down anymore. I don't know what lies ahead of me. I know it'll be hard, but I have the capability to succeed. I just need to work on wanting it for myself, not for anyone else. That's what I have trouble with. I need to learn how to get motivation from within. It's hard to feel inspired and spiritual when

I'm inside all the time. I'd like to look at some pictures of Moab & Colorado. You need to know how much I love you with all my heart and appreciate everything you do for me. God couldn't have blessed me with a better mother. I love you Mom.

Little Lizzie

October 14, 2005: Letter from Straight & Narrow

Dear Mommy,

Thank you for all the thoughtful things you sent me. I got the package on Wednesday. It really meant a lot to me, I was jumping up and down with excitement! I'm glad the letter I sent you made you happy. I feel kind of at a standstill. This medication is keeping me in a good mood, but it's almost like it's not natural. I remember always being sort of sad since I was pretty small. This is so foreign to me. I just watched "Message in a Bottle," the movie based on the Nicholas Spark book. It reminded me of Matt, and I almost cried many times. I used to cry at anything. I really just want to let all the bad stuff out. What do you suggest? I'm sorry I missed your birthday & didn't get you anything and I was a brat. All the flowers I drew on the front of this envelope are from the *Wildflowers of the Rockies* book you sent. Was that mine? It looks familiar. You can tell my memory's still shot. How did you know I wanted a flower book?

It's Saturday now and I've been here 20 days. Being honest I definitely still have reservations about using. I still love getting high. I go to church twice a week and I've been praying that God will take away my obsession and cravings. I was ready to leave Straight & Narrow with my friend last night after church. I took an extra Seroquel I saved, and thank God it made me too tired to leave, like I'd hoped it would. I'm glad I'm still here. After 28 days I'll be able to listen to the music I want for a half an hour, please, please, please send Gorillaz & Gwen Stefani. My favorite rap song is by Three Six Mafia called "Stay Fly." You should download it. They don't really play it much up here in north jersey bc it's west coast apparently – but we heard it all the time on BET in jail & I've been waiting to hear it since then & finally it came on this morning.

I hope you like the picture I drew you. Everyone saw it and now I have to make at least 5 more for people. I've been waiting to see the doctor for over a week since I was told I have hep C.

If I'm at a progressed stage of the disease, I'll need treatment. It's very expensive & they won't do it here. I love you so much Mommy! I miss you. Hopefully I'll talk to you soon.

Love, Elizabeth

Worksheet November 10, 2005: Straight & Narrow

How aware are you of your emotions?

HAPPY: List five things that you usually respond to with joy or pleasure.
1. sex
2. music
3. traveling
4. the ocean
5. shopping
6. my brother

SAD: List five things you usually respond to with sorrow, tears, or a sense of loss.
1. my [half] sisters
2. Matt

3. wasted opportunities
4. my mom's illness
5. my distancing myself from my family, missing their lives, firsts of my little brother

ANGER: List five things that you usually respond to with anger.
1. dad
2. boyfriend
3. family not understanding my mom
4. when I think about giving up my way out of Jersey (college)
5. [stepbrother] being treated better than me or my half-siblings

FEAR: List five things that you usually respond to with fright.
1. staying clean
2. dad's anger
3. failure
4. being alone
5. my mom's stability or lack thereof

EXCITEMENT: List five things that you usually respond to with a sense of curiosity & energy.
1. new places
2. beauty in the world & other people
3. opportunity to prove myself
4. new relationships
5. connecting with people

CONTENTMENT: List five things that you usually respond to with a sense of comfort and calm.
1. music
2. my mom (sometimes)

3. [stepbrother]
4. snowboarding
5. reading
6. nature

LOVE: List five things that you usually respond to with a warm sense of intimacy and affection.
1. Matt
2. mom
3. [stepbrother]
4. [cousin]
5. Cheryl [Florida rehab roommate]

December 1, 2005: Letter from Straight & Narrow

Hey Mommy!

I hope you're doing well. I love you and miss you. I wish I was out there in Moab with you and Livvy [my cat]. Just had a good conversation with [stepmom] and I'm pretty happy – that really made my day. I tried Daddy's cell and said "hi" then got cut off, and you know how technologically impaired he is, the voicemail wasn't set up, so I'll try again Monday.

I hope you're happy. I'm glad you're going to the library a lot. I'm writing with the pretty pink sparkly pen you sent. I forgot to tell you how much I like it and everyone else wants it. I'm really doing good here. I wake up happy, my cravings are negligible, and my anxiety is getting better. The wonders of psych medicine, maybe.

I finished the Courtney Love book in a day & a half. I can have any candy as long as it's not gum and it's in the original package. The bulk candy is a good value instead of bars. You pretty much know what I like (all chocolate, just not mint). I like "Gold Digger" too. Okay, I have to go to group now. I Love You! I Miss You!

Love, Your Baby Girl, Lizabuf

December 16, 2005: Letter from Straight & Narrow

Hey Mama!

I love you! Thank you so much for the Christmas &
birthday presents! I felt so special getting all those
packages. Hopefully Daddy & [stepbrother] are coming to
visit me tomorrow. It had been snowy the past couple of
weekends, but it got sunny today and it all melted, at least
it's warmer so I can enjoy going out to smoke.

Being a good girl has its advantages – I've been picked
to go to 2 college basketball games, 2 plays, a concert w/
70's soul groups, caroling at a nursing home, and the most
enjoyable (I told you I joined the Black church, right?) was
an outing with the women from the church. We went to the
Holiday Inn in Newark. It was a luncheon and the Secretary
of State of NJ gave a speech. (I forgot to tell you I dyed &
highlighted my hair, it's darker, still w/blonde – at first it
was orange & I cried but now it looks good). We got to eat
really good food including: Portuguese rolls, salad w/ good
dressing, yummy baked chicken w/ excellent gravy, roasted
red potatoes & vegetables, delicious cheesecake w/
chocolate sauce, good coffee, and a Ferrero Rocher. It was
really special. We all felt like normal people. Oh and a cute
waiter had this girl at the desk give me his number and said
please call. Of course I didn't, but it gave me a little
confidence.

It is hard though to weigh what I do now. My friend is
skinny & blonde & works out all the time and you know
how lazy I am. I've gotta accept that I'm not meant to be
100 lbs. My counselor Lauryn said she's gonna buy a book
that will be perfect for me – she wants to deal with my
weight & confidence issues. It feels good doing positive

31

things. I'm starting to want more for myself and understanding I'll never be perfect or live up to expectations I felt Dad had of me. I do want to complete college though.

I'm really content here, I'm trying to find out who I am and be happy with me and believing that it's ok not to have a boyfriend. I do know that I have a lot of work to do still and I know this isn't going to be easy. I think about how shy I used to be, I broke out of that when guys started paying attention to me. Now I know that I don't need drugs or guys to be outgoing. I'm not afraid of everything and everyone anymore. I've dealt with jail and here and people like me. I don't need anything but myself.

I'm so lucky to have you for my mommy. I'm not afraid to tell you stuff (for the most part), especially now that I'm trying this honesty thing on for size. I want you to be happy and I want to make you proud like I think I used to. I forgot that I used to be good at things I put my mind to (like clarinet and spelling). I need to put that drive back in my life. My best friend here is perfect (in my eyes anyway), blonde, skinny, gorgeous. I don't see anything but fat when I look in the mirror and I know I need to exercise to change that, but it's hard. I don't have the energy. I'm just trying to like myself and not focus on my body, but you know what that's like for me.

I love you Mommy so much. I hope you have a good Christmas. I'll be thinking about you & missing you for my birthday breakfast – watching "A Christmas Story," ("You'll shoot your eye out") – it's just weird not having you w/ me like I used to. I guess I still haven't gotten used to it after almost 4 years. I'm so lucky to have you. I'm sorry I've let you down. I just hope I can make up for it and make people believe in me again. Oh my god I say that but I go back and forth about belief in myself. I'm just so fucking fixated on my appearance! I don't know, I'll be thinking about you at 9:18am on my birthday, thank you for

32

giving me life and just being a wonderful mother. I wish I could call you on Christmas. At least I'm not where I was last year, at the [motel], alone. I'll love you forever, I'll like you for always!

Love, Your Little Lizzie
PS Please send my prom pics so I can see me pretty.

December 21, 2005: Letter from Straight & Narrow

I love you Mommy!

Here's a little bit about where I'm at. I was feeling good for a while, seeing people smoking crack in movies and not wanting to go back there. Then recently I've been real grouchy and I watched a movie today about men in a sober house, they were doing good then one guy relapsed and shot dope for the 1st time and died. At first I didn't feel anything, at least not in my stomach, but it kind of awakened my desire to be bad, evil, sick, addicted. I talked about it to my friends who were feeling the same way.

Then I realized that even though I like being that way, it's no comparison to being happy and free. I remembered going to the Ben Harper concert with Kristen this summer. I smoked crack before she picked me up and the drive there was unbearable, then we got there and it was incredible. It was genius and beautiful and I felt like a person again. I talked and identified with Kristen and wanted to get clean. Then when I got home Bob had more crack. I couldn't help myself when it's right in front of me and the feeling when there was none left was horrible and I felt like complete shit.

I'm trying to write more and talk myself out of those bad thoughts, but sometimes I feel like a phony. I feel like this happy person is not the real me because all I remember ever feeling is like a dejected, unsure loser. I also find myself hating people for no apparent reason, other than the way they look bothers me. I hope I can talk to you soon Mom.

Love, Liz

December 23, 2005: Letter from Straight & Narrow

Hey Mama,

I just got the collage you sent. It was so thoughtful! It made me smile and cry. I know you put a lot of time into it and I want you to know how good it made me feel, even the packaging was pretty (as usual). Everyone here loved it, especially the messages of encouragement. You put everything I liked on it, thank you for knowing all the little things I like, it was my favorite present, Mommy! I hope your xmas is good. Today we went to the main Straight & Narrow place & got presents (people donated clothes & toys). I got a light jacket, white tees, a bra, stationary & they let me have a Gund teddy bear for my brother (it plays music).

I was so happy to talk to you yesterday. I'm doin' ok. 2 ½ months to go. In a few days I'll have 5 months clean. Thank you for the sweet & encouraging card. Can you send the Will Ferrell dvd w/ "more cowbell" please?!? We could use the laughs here. Dad & [stepbrother] will visit on January 14th. I miss you and thank God every day for the special & beautiful Mommy he gave me. I love you bunches!

Longer Letter Later, Love, Little Lizzie

January 19, 2006: Worksheet Straight & Narrow

Coping With Loss

Things to Change:
- My need to always be in a relationship
- My low motivation in school
- My desire to be bad
- My wanting to fit in
- Not expressing my emotions to some family members
- I want to be a role model for [stepbrother]
- My negative thinking
- My feeling I am missing out on outside things while I am in here
- Liking depression
- I need to accept my mom's illness
- My obsession with my appearance

Things Not to Change
- My creativity
- My positive thinking, idealism
- When I'm silly
- My compassion

January 30, 2006: Letter from Straight & Narrow

Hi Mommy,

I'm feeling kinda depressed, especially when faced with the thought of eight more months here. [Elizabeth was originally told 6 months in Straight & Narrow; in January, they switched it to 12 months].

I've been thinking about cutting (I get obsessed with it but I've been talking about it to Lauryn [counselor] and in groups). Other people identify, but I still feel destructive. I don't mean to be depressing. I'm just hating this uncertainty. I'm anxious to start over and live my life and see you and everyone else. Sometimes I just feel so unnecessary, like I'm forgettable and an embarrassment and dad tells my brother I'm "in college."

I just wanna go far away so no one will see me when I screw my life up again. And I want to party like someone who's 21 should. I hate that I'm in this fucking "drug addict, college dropout, criminal" category now. And if I find someone for me, they'll have to be an addict because who else could accept my fucked up past. It's scary that I'm feeling this way because I had been doing pretty good and there's no reason for my feelings I'm not PMS-ing or anything.

I just wanna go home, but I don't have one. I still feel like a little girl, and I want my mommy and daddy. I miss Matt [soul mate] like nothing I've ever felt, I miss Cheryl [rehab roommate], I miss my memories – all my pictures are in Florida. How depressing, I can't look back at the innocent times. And I feel guilty for venting all this to you because you have your own problems to deal with and I want so bad for you to be happy. I haven't felt like writing and I finally do and it's this bullshit. I haven't had cigarettes for weeks; Dad gave me one pack that was gone in 2 days because I've been bumming them for so long.

I think so much & I end up bringing myself down even more. I miss you like crazy and I love you so much. I pray that you're happy every night and I wish I could come see you. I need to stop thinking negatively, but it's so hard. I just want to leave. I don't know what else to say. I miss you. I think happy memories of us and I feel a little better. I feel guilt and regret and I start thinking what if...? I feel like I'll never be successful, I'll always be owing money, too fat, not pretty. I'm gonna go & I hope this letter made you glad to hear from me like your packages make me, even if I'm a little down. I'll love you forever, I'll like you for always, as long as this lifetime, my mommy you'll be. (I know I didn't get the phrasing right, sorry).

Love, Little Lizzie

February 5-6, 2006: Straight & Narrow

Five days after she wrote the above letter, in which she mentioned talking to her counselor Lauryn about cutting, Elizabeth cut herself and was taken to the hospital and left in the psych ward overnight. Elizabeth woke up in the psych ward the next morning and called me, crying, because no one from Straight & Narrow was there with her. I spoke to the nurse, who said she was waiting to be seen by the psychiatrist. After she met with the psychiatrist, someone from Straight & Narrow picked her up. That afternoon, Elizabeth, her counselor Lauryn, and the director of Straight & Narrow had a meeting. They decided she needed to be transferred to a MICA (Mental Illness Chemical Abuse) facility.

February 7, 2006: Straight & Narrow

It was agreed that Elizabeth would be transferred to Saint Clare's Behavioral Health to enter a program for eating disorders and cutting.

That afternoon I called Elizabeth's counselor Lauryn and she was crying.

Elizabeth had just walked out of Straight & Narrow.

February 8, 2006

Evidently Liz had left with Lisa – whose boyfriend had smuggled crack, pills, and a cell phone into Straight & Narrow, inside of a shampoo bottle.

At 12:00am, Liz called me, she wouldn't say from where. She said she did not leave to use drugs, but that she was feeling agitated, suicidal, and had been cutting. She did not sound high, and she apologized for not calling me sooner. That afternoon Liz called again, this time obviously high. I suggested she try to get to Saint Clare's (where Straight & Narrow had planned to send her). She was crying about how much she had screwed up. Then she had to go because she needed to go inside where it was warm. She said she would try to call me tomorrow. I called and asked my dad, Elizabeth's pop-pop, if the next day he would go get her stuff at Straight & Narrow. Hopefully Liz would call, and her pop-pop could take her to Saint Clare's.

February 9, 2006

Elizabeth called me from a hotel. She was crying, and obviously high… "Mommy I'm hungry." I told her pop-pop was driving up to get her belongings from Straight & Narrow and he could come get her at the hotel. She gave me the name and location of the hotel. Soon my dad called me, and I relayed the message. My dad called an hour later and said he had found her sleeping on the hotel lobby's couch. Liz said Lisa bought her a room and left her there. Liz and pop-pop got lunch and then went to Saint Clare's. The hospital said she was no longer a psych emergency. Elizabeth and my dad sat there for seven hours and finally she was admitted to detox for 2 days. She had used heroin, crack, Percocet, Xanax, and Ativan during the past two days.

February 11, 2006: Saint Clare's Behavioral Health

My dad picked Elizabeth up.
Her diagnosis: Poly-substance Dependence.

38

Elizabeth had an intake scheduled at a nearby rehab. There wouldn't be a warrant issued by Pretrial Intervention if she went directly into MICA (Mental Illness Chemical Abuse) treatment.

February 11, 2006: Summit Oaks Hospital

Liz was assessed and admitted to Summit Oaks Hospital. She asked me not to tell her Dad about her relapse. Elizabeth told me she had used crack and pills while in Straight & Narrow.

Diagnoses at Summit Oaks:
- Hepatitis C
- Heroin dependence
- Cocaine dependence
- Bipolar disorder

Medications prescribed at Summit Oaks:
- Wellbutrin
- Buspar
- Seroquel

Third Rehab

February 20, 2006: Summit Oaks Hospital in N.J. to C.A.R.E. Rehab in Florida

On February 20th 2006, after 9 days, Elizabeth was discharged from Summit Oaks Hospital to attend C.A.R.E. in South Florida.

Discharge Planning Special Instructions:

If Bulimia resumes – patient should discontinue Wellbutrin immediately to prevent seizure risk.

February 28, 2006: Letter from C.A.R.E. Rehab, Florida

Hey Mommy!

I miss talking to you as often as I was able to at Summit Oaks. My counselor gave me the message you told her. Thank you for being here for me like you always have! I'm really happy here. They didn't give me any of the meds on my prescription, but I feel surprisingly good for the moment. Since I've been here, I haven't had any anxiety worth mentioning.

Oh my God Mom, Matt's [soul mate] grandma just walked into the AA meeting. Oh forget what I said about anxiety. I'm shaking now. I don't know if I'm ready for this. She smiled and said "hi," and I saw a look of recognition. There was still 20 min left of the meeting, so I waited (not too patiently) and then I went over to her. I said "Hi ____, I'm Elizabeth. I was in Behop [Behavioral Health of the Palm Beaches] w/ Matt a while back." She said "Oh, that's where I know you from, I was trying to place you." I asked how Matt was doing, she said he was still out there using and the progression has been bad. She asked me how long I've been clean. I told her the abridged, cleaned up version. She said it was a disaster after he came back from Jersey. Then she said that "if you & he are meant to be I know your paths will cross again." She wished me well. I told her I'd continue to pray for Matt.

I guess it was good that I found out that Matt's alive. I knew that he'd still be using. I just wish so much that things would have been different. I had the worst feeling when he left Florida with that guy Rich. It was like I knew it would end up this way. I didn't know what to do with myself that day. I just lay in bed reading his letters and looking at his pictures and wearing his T shirt. After he was gone for a half hour, he came back to give me one last kiss and I felt so much better. You know I'll never let myself get over Matt.

> I have wings
> I'm 1,000 miles away
> from the pain.
> In the sea
> the depths bring me back to you
> and we float.
> To the sky
> can't reach any further now
> see me fly.
> In the dark
> my breath is caught
> at the sight
> of your face.

I want the best for Matt, and I know that while I'm here I won't concern myself with his whereabouts but I can't promise that after I get my shit together I won't try to find him. It's been hard coming to all the same meetings that I went to with Matt. We drove by our old apt. and by me and Cheryl's street. One night after a meeting we took a scenic drive along the ocean and then took a cigarette break at the parking lot of the last beach I went to with Matt. I haven't run into anyone else I knew from down here, kind of depressing but I guess that relapse rate is true – or hopefully they all just moved away.

Things having to do with the guys here are driving me nuts – nothing happened, only a fucking conversation, and it's like this huge deal and everyone's looking at me and talking to me like "you're so bad." But like Jesus, I'm not here because I'm a fucking angel. Believe me, I could go much further, I have at every other rehab. Now it's going to be addressed and wah wah boo hoo. And even though I haven't said a word to this guy or even looked his way today, my roommate says I need to watch it or the other residents are going to be forced to have a fucking intervention over it. Where am I? I know I'm not at church camp but it's expected by other crack heads and dope fiends to act like it and magically have willpower after just 5 goddamn days here.

Love, Lizzie

March 9, 2006: Letter from C.A.R.E. Rehab, Florida

Hey Mama!

It's Thursday night. Tomorrow is my individual w/ Shelly so hopefully I'll be able to call you. I'm still doing really well. I'm beginning to like who I am, slowly mind you. I still hate my body but I know that if I stay healthy I can change it for the right reasons and in the right way. Oh there's no music therapy here, that was a lie, but I'm enjoying myself & I feel positive. I'm looking to the future in a good way and I feel really wonderful today. It's like I'm smiling on the inside and I wanna be a better person and stop isolating myself from people who love me. I'm tired of seeking approval of others. I want to approve of myself. I just want to jump up and down, dance & sing, and give you a big hug Mom! You've been my biggest support. I wanna be there for you. I know we can have a great relationship especially now that I'm seeing my bratty ways for what they were.

I think I'm gonna stay down here. There's so much support. I don't want to run back to Jersey because I'm scared of being alone. I know I can make it. I'm smart. I can make friends and I've got to work up the courage to get a sponsor. I'm so lucky to be alive, not in prison or with a needle in my arm or a crack pipe to my lips slowly killing my spirit and destroying my body and what little respect I had for myself. I'm learning so much. We go to a lot of the same meetings that I went to at Behop [Behavioral Health of the Palm Beaches rehab]. I don't remember ever listening to anyone speak at those, I just fooled around with my friends and stared at the clock. Now I listen to everyone speak and I get so much out of it. Even when people say stupid stuff, it keeps me aware of what not to do. I actually leave meetings feeling good and just a little more enlightened than when I walked in. I will say goodnight and watch the end of "the O.C." I love you more than anything Mommy! Be Happy Sheila Beila!

XOXO Your Little Lizzie

March 10, 2006 Letter from C.A.R.E. Rehab, Florida

Hey Mom, Shelly had me sign a contract that reads as follows:

> I, Elizabeth, will not harm myself in any way while a resident at C.A.R.E. This includes mutilating myself by cutting my skin or by any other means of self-harm. I agree to immediately alert my counselor Shelly if I have any thoughts of hurting myself. If my counselor is unavailable, I will immediately alert the staff in charge. I also agree to keep a diary of any thoughts of wanting to hurt myself and the reasons why. I will share this journal with my counselor at the beginning of each appointment while at C.A.R.E.

What do you think about this?

Oh, and I met w/ the psychiatrist, Shelly, & the clinical director about my PMS and they refused to put me on birth control. They gave me 5 natural pills called 5HTP or something to that effect. They said it'd be like giving me permission to have sex. (Like lack of protection really stops a sex addict). Anyway I was still not in a good mood and I had bad cramps but I was aware of why I was feeling that way so it was bearable. Whatever.

Love, Liz

April 11, 2006: Letter from C.A.R.E. Halfway House, Florida

Hey Mama!

I'm sorry I haven't written. I've been so busy since I moved to the halfway house. At first I was nervous but now

I'm loving it. Just being on Singer Island is relaxing. I've got 2 really great roommates. We've all got a lot in common – eating disorders and one girl used to cut, so it's a great supportive vibe and I feel like I can talk about anything with them.

I saw Kristen this weekend. She looks great! I encouraged her to attend the eating disorder anonymous meeting that I go to on Monday nights. It's been a little hard to keep up w/ eating right over here. I have subconsciously been restricting because of lack of fitting clothes but I'm being honest and getting good feedback from the other girls.

Are you doing anything for Easter? I think we're going to a non-denominational service on Sunday morning. I can't tell you how happy I am here. I mean I'm a normal person, I have bad times, but I don't stay stuck, I talk about it. I'm finding that over here I've got time to journal and read more. I'm in acupuncture now, I'll call you tonight!

Love, Little Lizabeth

April 24, 2006: C.A.R.E. Inpatient Rehab, Florida

Elizabeth was "sent back" to C.A.R.E. inpatient rehab for having sex with Matt [soul mate] and attending an "outside" AA barbeque without permission.

May 8, 2006 Elizabeth's Private Journal at C.A.R.E. Rehab, Florida

What Liz wants:

to be sober and free
to be peaceful and serene
to not be "normal" or ordinary
	a little edgy in dress & style

questioning societal norms, searching for my own
answers
    free to speak my mind
not be afraid to be "wrong"
healthy sexual relationships
    if I feel good and filled w/ well being
    practice safe sex
    fidelity for the time being
    doing only what I want to do, respect
    listening to my intuition about partner choice
go back to school and explore career possibilities
    actually go to class and accept/experience learning
as a gift
    interact w/and enjoy other students without party
life being the main focus
    going for myself, not others' expectations
independent, adult to adult relationship w/ Mom
have a relationship w/ Dad outside of "Daddy's World"

May 14, 2006: C.A.R.E. in Florida to Axel's home in Texas

Elizabeth and Axel [future husband] are kicked out of
C.A.R.E. for fraternization. Elizabeth flew with Axel to his
home in Texas.

Marriage and Fourth Rehab

July 23, 2006: Mexico

On July 23, 2006, Elizabeth's dad called and told me
that Liz and Axel took a cruise ship from Florida to
Mexico, jumped ship, and stayed in Mexico. Liz called a
few days later. She was crying, "Do you hate me?" She
thought she might be pregnant. Axel was drinking, Liz was
using drugs and they were fighting.

August 13, 2006: Mexico

When Elizabeth called me the next time, she was
paranoid. She said "don't tell grammy or pop-pop where I
am. They might send bounty hunters since they won't get
their bail money back." She was definitely pregnant plus
she had a serious infection. She and Axel were still
fighting. Liz begged me to come to Mexico to bring her
back to the U.S.

I arrived in Cancun and took a bus to the fishing village
of Mahahual, where Elizabeth and Axel lived by the water.
When I arrived, Liz and Axel were in their shack, fighting.
Elizabeth and I got on the bus back to Cancun. Axel
followed. Liz split her time between my seat and Axel's
seat. In Cancun, Axel got a room at our hotel. We had three
days until our flight to Colorado. Again, Elizabeth split her
time between hanging out with me, and hanging out with
Axel.

49

I emailed my family that Axel seemed calm, but Elizabeth seemed volatile. When the three of us were in Axel's room watching MTV, Elizabeth thought Axel was staring at the dancers. She was very jealous and lashed out. I was later told that someone was supplying Liz with crack while we were at the hotel, but I didn't witness anything, so I'm not certain.

August 17, 2006: Denver, Colorado Airport

Elizabeth and I got on the plane to Denver. When we got off the plane, there was a cop waiting for her. The Denver police had been notified that she was on the plane, and that she had an outstanding warrant in New Jersey. The warrant was for a missing court appearance. I told the cop that I was her mother, she was pregnant, and I would make sure her legal issues were taken care of. He let her go. Elizabeth's Uncle Jim and Aunt Debbie picked us up.

August 18, 2006: Moab, Utah

Elizabeth moved into my one-bedroom apartment in Moab. Liz had used cocaine during her early pregnancy in Mexico. She had a serious unidentified infection or microbe. Although Elizabeth really wanted the baby, for those reasons, she had an abortion. It was awful. Elizabeth had an allergic reaction to one of the medications. She regretted the abortion and obsessed over her lost baby for months – the clinic gave her the remains of the fetus in a container.

Before and after the abortion, Elizabeth had been in pain. We went to the doctor at least three times because of her infection/microbe. The doctor gave her pain pills to last several days. Eventually the doctor stopped giving Liz pain pills. Elizabeth was fine with that. She had gotten a waitressing job at a local pizzeria, and she was making good money in tips. She met a boyfriend who used heroin. Once Elizabeth started using heroin in Moab, things went downhill quickly.

About a month later, Elizabeth and I visited my brother and sister-in-law in Colorado. It was obvious that I was a mess from the stress of sharing a one-bedroom apartment with Elizabeth. We all talked and agreed that Elizabeth would go to South Carolina with her aunt and uncle. They had sold their Colorado house and were moving to South Carolina the next month.

October 7, 2006: South Carolina

Elizabeth moved to South Carolina with her aunt and uncle. They drug tested her several times and she had no drugs in her system. Elizabeth got her wisdom teeth out and did not misuse the pain pills. She started seeing a therapist that she liked and had an appointment to see a doctor for her Hepatitis C. Liz was getting her school transcripts sent so she could take college classes.

Undated Poem by Elizabeth

Dear Elizabeth
at this moment
I have chosen
you to mean
everything to me

Sheila's Journal December 2, 2006

I'm extremely pissed at Elizabeth. She called yesterday about her "baby." When she was living with me in Moab, she obsessed over the remains. She eventually agreed to give the container to my therapist, M, whom Liz had seen several times. I reminded Liz that she had promised M she

51

wouldn't look at the remains – Liz said it didn't matter what she had told M. I told her I absolutely would not mail the remains.

On Elizabeth's MySpace page, it says she is "in a relationship." I know she's communicating with Axel by email – maybe by phone as well. Today I threatened to tell Jimmy and Debbie. I said that she was taking advantage of them, abusing their trust. Liz said she wouldn't talk to me about it; she would discuss it with her therapist. I said she'd break Debbie's heart. She hung up.

December 15, 2006: South Carolina to Las Vegas

It was my brother Jimmy's 40th birthday. My brother, sister-in-law, and Elizabeth all flew to Las Vegas. In Las Vegas, Elizabeth disappeared. My brother and sister-in-law were frantic. It turned out that Elizabeth and Axel had secretly planned to meet up in Las Vegas and get married.

2007

About five months after they were married, Elizabeth and Axel were delighted to discover that Elizabeth was pregnant. When she was several months pregnant, Elizabeth almost lost the baby due to a sub-chorionic hemorrhage. After she was cleared medically, she went to rehab for a month. Her diagnoses there were PTSD, depression, and anxiety. Because she was pregnant, they did not put her on medication.

August 11, 2007: Letter from Rehab when pregnant

Hey Mama!

Hope all is well in beautiful Moab! So this place is, um, worse than Straight & Narrow. Didn't think it could be but, it's just dirty here. My room is ewww. I just want to disinfect the whole place. Apparently we're lucky if we go to one outside meeting a week. I've yet to meet my counselor but I hear she's a judgmental bitch who knows nothing about addiction. Yeah! So it looks like I'll be here to complete the program sans any real therapy. The groups suck – I think I could run my own rehab on all the recovery knowledge I've collected better than these people can. Sorry I didn't write much, just want to say hi and I love you!

Love, Elizabeth

Baby

Elizabeth's Voicemail to Sheila September 22, 2007

"Hey Mama, I was just hoping you had your cell phone on, I hope everything's going good there. I miss talking to you a whole bunch! I guess if you can, email me or turn your phone on sometimes. I always try calling, so…..Leave it on I'll eventually get ahold of you. Alright, I love you, bye"

Elizabeth's Email to Sheila October 29, 2007

hey mama

just wanted to let u know that i can't read that hello kitty email u sent bc i'm not downloading anything to this computer bc we've been having problems with it, oh well. i hope ur having a good day. i tried calling earlier but u must be at an appointment or something. also auntie meghan said she emailed me pics but i never got them so could u please forward them to me? also remind me to give the address and info to type in so u can go online and access our family portrait pics, [Elizabeth, Axel, and his 3 kids] they're awful cute. ok, well i guess i'll try calling u in a minute. by the way, try to think of an email address for me that's not corny. love you, hope ur having a lovely monday! love your darling daughter

Riley was born in the fall of 2007. Elizabeth was so happy.

January 16, 2008: Children's Hospital

Elizabeth called me and said, "now don't freak out." Elizabeth and Axel had taken Riley to his pediatrician. He told them to take Riley to the hospital, he had RSV (respiratory syncytial virus). Riley was put on a bunch of monitors, his nose was suctioned, his lungs x-rayed and suctioned of mucus. He was fed intravenously and his monitors were closely watched at the nurse's station.

January 19, 2008: Pediatric Intensive Care

Elizabeth called me at 5:am, they had to take baby Riley by ambulance to a different children's hospital, where he was in pediatric intensive care with a bunch of other babies hooked up to machines. Elizabeth gave me a number and code to call to get updates on him.

February 3, 2008

Baby Riley was released from the hospital, had seen his own pediatrician, and things were fine.

Elizabeth's Voicemail to Sheila February 28, 2008, 2:08am

"I wanted to let you know it appears I'm being fucking committed. So, you know, I just wanted to let you know. I love you. I didn't try to kill myself. You understand what I'm fucking going through. Nobody else does. So don't call the house looking for me. I'm at Medical Center in Independence, Texas. Isn't that a fucking joke. Don't call anyone else, okay. Just call here and ask for me. I love you, goodnight." [Elizabeth had cut herself so they took her to the medical center. She was not suicidal so they released her].

Elizabeth's Facebook profile: early 2008

Basic Information:
Networks: New Jersey
Sex: Female
Relationship Status: Married
Interested in: Men/Women
Looking for: Friendship. Networking

Activities: yoga, reading, playing with my son, MUSIC!!!!!, dancing, scrapbooking, movies, BEACH!!!, writing, snowboarding

Interests: family, friends, the beach, music, photography, yoga, graphic design, fashion, all types of art....trying to get my own business started

Favorite Music: Ben Harper, Bob Marley, Damien Marley, Mazzy Star, Johnny Cash, Tool, APC, Rage Against the Machine, The Eagles, Portishead, Led Zeppelin, The Mars Volta, Tom Petty, Janis Joplin, The Beatles, Pharrell, Nirvana, Sublime, Red Hot Chili Peppers, Gorillaz, Hed PE, Fleetwood Mac, Amy Winehouse, Wu-Tang Clan, Mos Def, Alice in Chains, David Bowie, Fiona Apple, Jack Johnson, HIM, Sigur Ros, NIN, Flyleaf, Billie Holiday, Incubus, STP, L'il Wayne, Iggy Pop, Lou Reed, G. Love & Special Sauce, The Rolling Stones, The Police, Mason Jennings, Tupac, Massive Attack.......the list goes on forever

Favorite TV Shows:

Real Time w/Bill Maher, No Reservations w/Anthony
Bourdain, WEEDS, Entourage, UFC, dirt, Prison Break,
Breaking Bad, Law & Order: Criminal Intent, Family Guy,
yo gabba gabba...

Favorite Movies:
Natural Born Killers, 21 Grams, SNATCH, lock, stock,
& 2 smoking barrels, BLOW, Fear & Loathing in Las
Vegas, The Lost Boys, Requiem for a Dream, Traffic, Rules
of Attraction, Dazed & Confused, Chocolat, The Princess
Bride, Pulp Fiction, Reservoir Dogs, True Romance,
Clerks, Mallrats, Garden State, Suicide Kings, Message in a
Bottle...

Favorite Books:
TAO TE CHING, The Catcher in the Rye, A Million
Little Pieces, anything by Chuck Palahniuk, Brett Easton
Ellis, Hunter S. Thompson, Jack Keruoac, Ann Rice,
Bridge to Terabithia, Bunny's Bath Time, The Runaway
Bunny...

Favorite Quotations:
"I want to rock your gypsy soul." [Van Morrison]

"I'm just see-through faded, super-jaded, OUT OF MY
MIND." [Alice in Chains]

"You are not a beautiful and unique snowflake." [Chuck
Palahniuk]

"I'll love you forever, I'll like you for always, as long as
I'm living, my baby you'll be" [*Love You Forever* by
Robert Munsch]

Member of Groups:

Addicted to Entourage, Philosophy is Sexy, Creative
Writing Group, Poetic Photography, Cyan Images, Music is
my drug...YES! It is an addiction, Why is suicide and self-
injury (i.e. cutting) taken as a joke?, Child Abuse
Awareness, Yoga Addicts, Namaste, Today!, Yoga Pose,
Drink or Sex Position, Universal Tao System, Addicted to
Travelling!, Fuck this...I'm Going to Hogwarts, Disney
Magic is My Favorite, I am Sexually Attracted to Talent,
A.R.S.E.N.A.L., Addiction Recognition Strength
Endurance Now And Life

Elizabeth's Facebook Status April 23, 2008: is with the
family

Elizabeth's Facebook Status April 24, 2008: "God grant
me the serenity to accept the things I cannot change, the
courage to change the things I can, and the wisdom to know
the difference."

Elizabeth's Facebook Status April 26, 2008: is chill ;)

Elizabeth's Facebook Status April 29, 2008: is needing
sleep...wild Riley is teething

Elizabeth's Facebook Status May 1, 2008, 2:15pm: is
"want what you have & you'll have what you want"

Elizabeth's Facebook Status May 1, 2008, 10:43pm: is
currently in the path of a tornado; thank God for four-level
houses w/basements

May 3, 2008

A letter arrived for Elizabeth. She had a court date of May
15th 2008 in New Jersey to review her Pretrial Intervention
case. She had violated Pretrial Intervention terms by being
kicked out of C.A.R.E. rehab in May 2006.

Elizabeth was currently diagnosed with postpartum depression and generalized anxiety disorder. She had been prescribed Lexapro [antidepressant] and Klonopin [benzodiazepine for anxiety, Elizabeth's most effective prescription medication].

Elizabeth's Facebook Status May 6, 2008: is preparing to face the music; 9 days and counting

Elizabeth's Facebook Status May 9, 2008: is dreading May 15th......

Elizabeth's Facebook Post May 15, 2008, 2:05am: is "I said Goddamn!!! Goddamn." [quote from the movie *Pulp Fiction*]

Elizabeth's Facebook Post May 15, 8:30am: is omg omg omg omg omg............ nervous, anxious and freaked out.

Elizabeth flew out and went to the case conference. She was re-admitted to the Pretrial Intervention program. When she returned from New Jersey, all hell broke loose. Axel planned to fly Elizabeth back to New Jersey, because he believed she had cheated on him while she was in New Jersey for the case conference.

May 21, 2008: Elizabeth's Private Journal – Flying to New Jersey

First the plane ticket was too expensive & Axel wasn't going to pay for it. Then he said he'd get me a bus ticket, when I was w/o any $ or any way to call my family. Finally, w/75cents to my name, no one to help me w/all my luggage, I stopped in the bar & had a drink. Eventually Axel came back & we had a few drinks together while looking for flights. We couldn't find any so we said goodbye to Riley and we got a hotel room. Everything was ok, we talked, periodically he'd get mad about the pizza delivery boy bc he thought I had cheated.

Back in New Jersey

May 23, 2008

Pretrial Intervention drug test positive for THC, amphetamines, benzos, and cocaine

May 28, 2008

Pretrial Intervention drug test positive for THC, amphetamines, benzos, and cocaine

Elizabeth's Facebook Status May 28, 2008: is trying.......

May 29, 2008

Pretrial Intervention drug test positive for THC and benzos

Elizabeth's Facebook Status May 31, 2008: is going to hell if she doesn't change her ways.......

Elizabeth's Facebook Status June 3, 2008: is back from the beach

Elizabeth's Facebook Status June 4, 2008: is working....... [local restaurant]

Elizabeth's Facebook Status June 5, 2008, 4:30pm is having dinner with my grandparents

Elizabeth's Facebook Status June 5, 2008, 7:49pm is pure evil

June 5, 2008

Elizabeth is arrested and charged with:
- Possession Marijuana Less than 50 Grams
- Possession Prescription Legend Drug, one Percocet pill

(These are both Disorderly Person Offenses)

Elizabeth's Facebook Status June 7, 2008: is WTF?!?

June 12, 2008: Elizabeth's Private Journal – New Jersey

Riley, my loving bunny boy:

Your mommy has made many mistakes in her life, that's why we're not together right now. No matter what Daddy says, I love you more than anything in this whole wide world. I am an addict, your father is an alcoholic. That is how we met, at rehab. You and I have been apart for three weeks…it feels like a lifetime. It's easier now for Mommy just to get high and forget about life & all the problems she's caused; but without my Riley, I feel like I'm dying inside. I'm trying to do everything I can to get you back in my arms honey-bunny. I keep pictures of you on me all the time, in case I'm tempted to do something that would keep you from me any longer. I sang to you on the phone 2 nights ago. I've been singing it since you were in Mama's belly. (To the tune of "Edelweiss") It goes:

Riley boy, Riley boy
every morning you greet me
soft & bright, clean & white
you look happy to meet me
BLOSSOM OF LOVE

May you bloom & grow
bloom & grow forever!
Riley boy, Riley boy,
You're my bunny forever!

The whole time you were in my belly, it was just you &
me. Until you were six months old, it was just you & me.
(Daddy was in diving school). I hope one day you'll
forgive me for letting my addiction come between me &
my angel. When you were in my belly for 3 months, you
almost died. I prayed to God & talked to you & told you to
hang in there. I asked God to give me my beautiful boy. I
called Pastor Glenn the next morning & asked his
congregation to pray for you & me. The next day I went to
the hospital & you were still alive! When you were 2
months old, you got a really bad cold [respiratory syncytial
virus] & had to go into the hospital. You had to be put into
the pediatric intensive care unit because you went into
respiratory failure. I stayed by your side for almost 2
weeks. You had to be put to sleep, you had a machine
breathing for you, and tubes everywhere. Mommy was so
scared. All she wanted to do was hold you, see you open
your eyes, at least hear you cry. I would stand over your
little hospital bed & cry & pray & hold your little hand &
sing to you. When you finally woke up I was so happy! You
are the light of my life, and I need to get help so that I can
be the best mommy I can be for my little angel. I'll love
you forever, I'll like you for always, as long as I'm living,
my baby you'll be.

Terminated

Elizabeth received a letter dated June 11, 2008 saying
she was being terminated from Pretrial Intervention due to
3 positive drug tests in the end of May, and her June 5th

arrest for possession. Elizabeth was accepted to a Connecticut Rehab starting June 28th.

Fifth Rehab and Divorce

June 28, 2008: New Jersey to Connecticut Rehab

I drove Elizabeth up to rehab. It was a good trip. We stopped at Friendly's to get lunch and ice cream. When we were almost at the rehab, Elizabeth pulled out a needle and works and shot up heroin in the car. I was afraid the rehab would not accept her – because she was supposed to be detoxed. During the intake interview, as she was nodding off, Elizabeth said she was just sleepy. The admitting staff member knew what was going on and said it happened all the time. She got Liz some sort of energy/vitamin drink and soon I left. The rehab diagnosed her with postpartum depression and generalized anxiety disorder. The rehab took her once a week to the Susan B. Anthony Project for an appointment regarding women's issues and PTSD.

June 29, 2008: Elizabeth's Private Journal Connecticut Rehab

I keep staring at the eight pictures I have of Riley and I can't believe I ever put anything before the best thing that God ever gave me. This beautiful perfect little boy that was almost taken away from me twice, [sub-chorionic hemorrhage, respiratory syncytial virus] I should have realized how lucky I was. I took motherhood for granted and now all I want is to hear him cry, know that he's alright, wonder how many teeth he has, if he remembers me, if I'll ever have my little Wild Riley back in my arms.

With nothing left to cloud my mind, it's just overwhelming that I'll have to take so many steps to be a part of his life. I feel like everything would feel better if I just had my boy by my side. I was on my way to getting him back and I wasn't strong enough to just take the necessary steps. I let Axel's predictions come true. I was out on the streets smoking crack & shooting dope & selling myself – I know I'm better than that.

June 30, 2008: Elizabeth's Private Journal Connecticut Rehab

So at last night's meeting someone said "Life will give you more than you can handle, but not more than you & your higher power together can handle." It's been over 40 days since I've seen Riley and it's not getting any easier. I just keep thinking about other things until all my feelings build up and I feel like I'm going to explode from missing him so much.

Just talked to Axel & told him where I was, he said, "So you're right back where I met you." He wants me to sign the [separation] agreement. I don't know what to do. It makes me sick to my stomach to think of just signing every little stipulation that **HE** wants.

July 5, 2008: Elizabeth's Private Journal Connecticut Rehab

What is it about myself that I am unhappy/uncomfortable with/hate/want to change:

I think my unhealthy childhood attachment w/ [cousin] prevents me from sustaining relationships.

July 9, 2008: Elizabeth's Private Journal Connecticut Rehab

I'm sitting on top of Mount Canaan, with a gorgeous view, blueberries for the picking, a really good group of people, sun is shining… the weather is sweet. At the moment I feel at peace, I'm savoring every little detail. The breeze, the warm sun; this trip has made me feel God's presence and made me aware of all His gifts. A few minutes ago there was a dragonfly hanging around and it just felt like it was there for me. Being out here has really cleared my head… yes I still miss Riley more than words can say.

July 17, 2008: Elizabeth's Private Journal Connecticut Rehab

Guaranteed Sobriety
1. Pray in the morning – ask God to keep me clean, ask for help
2. Go to a meeting, get phone #'s, Step, Big Book Meeting
3. Read something spiritual, inspirational
4. Talk to another addict, preferably @ the sponsor level
5. Pray @ night, thank God for keeping me clean & sober that day

July 23, 2008: Connecticut Treatment Center

To Whom it May Concern:

Thank you for considering me for Senior Residency. I am so grateful to have this opportunity for recovery, and a new life through the programs here. Since coming here, I've been able to start the process of opening up to others and finding my true self. I believe that taking the next step in the Mind/Body/Spirit program will help me to become more responsible and provide me with the accountability of being held to a higher standard. Chairing the community meeting would be a good exercise in becoming more confident with speaking in groups, which I'll need when I attend 12-step meetings on the "outside." While sitting and journaling on Mt. Canaan, taking in all of God's gifts and feeling His presence, I was able to feel at peace and live in the moment. It definitely opened my eyes to the endless possibilities recovery has to offer me.

July 30, 2008 Elizabeth's Private Journal Connecticut Rehab

I just got caught with Evan.

I'd been feeling pretty bad all night, feeling guilty for contributing to the negativity in the community, not living up to everything I said in my Senior Residency letter, and for letting myself get caught up in something that took the focus off my recovery. I wrote a 4th step about it and it showed that I'd been justifying my behavior. I'm mad at myself because I'm so sick of these character defects, but yet I am still acting slutty, sneaky, selfish, dishonest, pleasure seeking, looking outside of myself for ways to feel better about myself. It's just a vicious cycle – like the drugs. My mistaken thinking was that this hasn't affected my recovery. Lately I've not been praying or writing my affirmations or calling my sponsor every night.

I know that sex is just another thing I'm powerless over and it's obviously made my life unmanageable. I was kicked out of two rehabs for the same thing and I should've learned with my marriage that this isn't the place to get involved with anyone. I want to be the best version of myself that I can be, stop living as a slave to drugs and sex and learn to be proud of who I am. I want to be respected and contribute something to the world. I want Riley to have a mother that he can look up to, I want to be there for him and give him all the love in the world, and show him a better life. I want to live up to the potential that everyone always said I had.

When I first came here, I said to myself that I wasn't going to do this here. I said I wasn't going to disrespect myself or sabotage my recovery again. The sex wasn't worth it – nothing is more important than what I have the chance to do here. Now I'll probably be kicked out and have to deal with the consequences, the shame of having to explain to my family why I lost this opportunity, that I wasted their help **AGAIN**, that I cared more about getting laid than about getting better and getting my son back. I know I need to stop beating myself up about my mistakes, but Joe said it best tonight, "How can you be so stupid, Elizabeth?" There I go again, fucking up every good thing that comes my way – and for what, Dave [counselor] is going to ask me tomorrow. WHY? And he'll get mad when I say I don't know why I do this shit. I'm sick and I know it. I need help. God, I need a miracle.

I really don't have the desire to use. That's how I know that recovery is possible. I asked God to remove the mental obsession and He did.

August 1, 2008: Kicked out of Connecticut Rehab, Home to New Jersey

Elizabeth called me, sobbing. She was being kicked out of the Connecticut rehab for fraternization, as she had expected. A "therapeutic" discharge. [**I sat next to Elizabeth when she had her intake interview. I specifically heard her tell the admitting staff member that she had a sex addiction**].

When Elizabeth got back to New Jersey, that night she went to a local bowling alley to score heroin and she got high. I didn't see Elizabeth or hear from her for the next six days. I was petrified. I knew her state of mind. Not only had she been abruptly kicked out of a rehab where she had felt safe, Elizabeth was desperately missing her baby, and had not had heroin in 35 days – her tolerance was gone so overdose was a risk.

August 7, 2008

Elizabeth did not show up for her August 7th court date – her official termination from Pretrial Intervention. I filed a missing person's report with the local police. That night the police found her. Elizabeth was medically evaluated and then processed at the county jail. There had been a warrant issued for her arrest due to her missed court appearance.

The next day I emailed the Connecticut rehab to tell them Elizabeth had been found. I suggested they might want to **seriously** re-think their policy regarding "therapeutic" discharges.

Jail

August 23, 2008: Letter from County Jail

Hey Mom!

Just wanted to say hi! I know I'm not the perfect daughter (note the lovely stationary, courtesy of the County Jail) but I must have done something right for God to bless me with a mother like you. Thank you for always being there and supporting me no matter what. Even though you annoy me to no end, I always have fun with you and I know I can tell you anything. Thanks for being you & I'm sorry I don't always treat you w/ respect. I can't wait to go out to eat, maybe I can make crème brulee for dessert. I miss you!

Love, Little Lizzie

September 3, 2008 Letter from County Jail – about to be bailed out

Dear Mama,

You didn't cause it,
You can't control it,
You can't cure it.

I'm staying with someone who doesn't use & who goes to meetings. I admitted that last time I had plans to use when I got out. It's different this time. I have a plan of action for relapse prevention, I am an adult, and you guys can't really want me to be locked up forever – or do you? I'm looking forward to spending lots of time with you. I even decided what I want to cook you for dinner if you'll let me. Sweet & sour chicken, snow peas, and my sticky coconut rice w/mango. Maybe you can teach me how to make that double ender cake for dessert.

I love you very much. It hurts that you think just because I want to get out of this lice-infested shithole that I want to use. That is not the case. I want to prove you all wrong. I'll show up for sentencing with a clean urine. I'm asking for your support when I get out, whether you think it's a good idea or not. I wasn't lying when I said you're my best friend. Please be there for me.

Love, Little Lizzie

September 5, 2008

Liz is bailed out and released from jail.

September 12, 2008

Arrested for Shoplifting, 4th Degree.

September 18, 2008: County Courthouse, Superior Court, Criminal

The friend who had bailed her out on September 5th requested that the judge revoke her bail because she was using substances. The judge agreed and Elizabeth was taken to jail.

September 24, 2008: Letter from County Jail

Hey Mommy,

I just wanted to thank you for that honest letter you sent. Yes it made me cry. I honestly don't know who this person inside me is anymore – I don't want to keep living this way because I know where it leads. I want to live a full happy life and be a good mother and wife, but everything just seems lost right now. Mom, you're all I've got in this world and I thank God every day for your faith, support & love.

I just want to be able to do the right thing, but you know that I feel normal w/ the drugs – the things I do for them & what it does to my family, I hate. I just feel so empty inside, like that smart, funny, creative, fun person is completely gone and all that's left is me, the Elizabeth everyone knows & looks at w/ pity & disappointment. I don't know what happened to me or what I can do to get myself back.

It already feels like I'll never have my Riley boy back, I should just give up & disappear and spare him the pain of having me in his life. That's all I've ever brought anyone who's ever known me if you think about it. Name one person whose life has not been made worse by me…I need you so much Ma, you know that, I don't know what I'd do w/out you… I just wish we could go away to Disney like when I was little and be silly again.

I don't know if the Elizabeth you know & love is still in here, if she is help her come back please. I wish your magic wand was real because this pain is only growing & this place is more miserable & hopeless by the minute.

I Love You and Miss You More Than You Know, Love, Lizzie

October 2, 2008: Letter from County Jail

Hey Mama,

I miss you so much. Let me tell you how much <u>more</u> I appreciate your support since Daddy visited. I didn't really realize how much he hurt me on Tuesday with what he said until I told you about it on the phone today and the tears came pouring down. Sometimes (most of the time) it feels like you're the only one who knows I can come out on top after all I've been through with my addiction. No matter what Daddy says, I do not define myself that way. I may have done some incomprehensible things, but that can't be how I view myself or I would end up being stuck doing that forever. I'm trying to love & forgive myself. I am a beautiful person who has a lot to offer the world & I know one day Riley will be proud of his mother.

I truly believe in the power of positive thinking and it helps to see your smiling face twice a week & all the nice things you send me. I felt like my world was crashing down after I got off the phone with Axel an hour ago. I made mistakes & I'm paying for them. But that doesn't mean I can't pick myself up and come back from this. I love you and I miss you and I can't wait to go to Disney World – with Riley hopefully, or it can just be a girls' vacation.

Love, Little Lizzie

October 11, 2008: Letter from County Jail

Hola Mama!

So I just went over the letter & yes you were right about the lady sentenced to four years & no I don't want to end up like that. I am continuing to seriously think about what I want to do for the rest of my life.

I've been thinking a lot about when Riley got sick. After that I had to be more fucked up than usual. That was a big test because I wanted to walk into the city & get high & I even had syringes w/ pain killers & benzos & I didn't touch them. But – I did take tons of pills & hid alcohol in my purse or ran out to the car to smoke weed when Axel was there.

You know what I just thought of that's comforting? My [step] brother was over 19 months when [stepmom] adopted him, so once I am back in Riley's life, it's not like there's no hope for bonding again. He grew inside me & I breastfed him, does that just become erased? I just looked over @ the new pictures of Riley & I am again dumbfounded at what a beautiful boy I have. Doesn't he have the most beautiful blue eyes you've ever seen? And what a smile! And those chubby little arms. I can't wait to see him, even if it's not for a while.

Love, Little Lizzie

"Elizabeth" October 29, 2008: Worksheet (County Jail)

Elizabeth
Daughter of [dad] and Sheila
Mother of Riley
Sister of [2 half-siblings] and [stepbrother]
Who is intelligent, creative, sensitive and compassionate.
Who likes yoga, surfing, dancing, cooking, traveling, and scrapbooking.
Who loves her family and most of all her beautiful son.
Who wants to be successful, the best mother she can be, married to someone she loves and who makes her happy, and content with the path she has chosen.
Who needs to follow a program of balanced living and recovery.

October 30, 2008: Letter from County Jail

Hey Mama!

It's Halloween, BOO-HOO! So I've been talking to this woman in here & she's trying to convince me to take drug court. She thinks that it will change my life like it did hers. (she's in here now for a false positive when she took a non-narcotic painkiller for á toothache). She thinks I'll have a better chance @ getting Riley if I'm in a structured program. What do you think?

When I get out of prison, I'm getting a tattoo. I've been thinking of Riley's name on the inside of my right wrist in case I ever feel like doing anything stupid. I also want a dragonfly & an evil girl w/ angel wings. All in good time. Maybe that can be my new addiction. I'm sure Dad will love that! Riley's gonna be a year soon. Can't believe it.

Love, Little Lizzie

November 12, 2008: Letter from County Jail

Mother Dearest,

Greetings from side cell. Thought I'd drop a quick postcard since you seem to think I intend to harm myself. It really pissed me off that you told the guards what you did. I'm <u>not at all</u> suicidal. I just like the song, the lyrics are beautiful & poignant. Just because someone has an appreciation for Sylvia Plath doesn't mean they'll stick their head in an oven. Furthermore, should I think that just bc you like Kurt Cobain & Nirvana that you'll become a heroin addict & blow your brains out? Now we both know you're smarter than that close-minded rationale.

I love you & thanks for the pictures. Love, Elizabeth

November 18, 2008: County Jail

Elizabeth had a romance with a young guard at the jail. Her bail was $10,000. He planned to help bail her out.

November 18, 2008: Elizabeth to Jail Guard on Inmate/Staff Correspondence paper

I thought for sure I'd be seeing you tonight. My mom came to visit & I convinced her to say it was "ok" for me to get out. Now I'm not sure if Mike will still bail me out. It sucks when you're not here. Maybe at least then I could get a kiss once in a while. What did my mom tell you about me? Do you still think I'm a sweet girl? I really like you & I hope you're for real. I've been waiting for someone to treat me right & I think I could make you happy. I'm so sick of guys just wanting me for sex.

November 19, 2008: Jail Guard to Elizabeth

Well hopefully I will see you? Will you leave with me or your Mom? I would be really upset if you left with Mike. Cuddling sounds really nice! Just want to be with you so bad! Please don't go home with him! Write me back. xxoo

November 20, 2008 Bailed Out of County Jail

The guard went to a bail bondsman and paid $1,000 to bail Elizabeth out. She came to my apartment, where we had dinner. That night the guard picked her up and they went out. They were pulled over. Both of them had been drinking, smoking weed or both. The next day the guard was fired – for bailing Elizabeth out.

Drug Court

December 12, 2008: Application to the Drug Court Program

Elizabeth had a court date and officially applied to drug court. A requirement of drug court was to have no violent charges. Elizabeth and Axel [her soon to be ex-husband] both had charges from an altercation at a bar in Texas, where Elizabeth had lived with Axel and baby Riley. Elizabeth had to resolve that charge in order to be admitted into drug court.

February 3, 2009: Resolving Legal Charge

My Dad flew out with Elizabeth to resolve her altercation charge at the Texas bar. Elizabeth and her pop-pop spent time with Axel and Riley. Riley was now 14 months old. Elizabeth had not seen him since he was 6 months old. In court, Elizabeth was put on unsupervised probation for two years and told not to frequent that bar. The charge was dropped.

That was the last time Elizabeth saw her son. The divorce decree specified that Elizabeth could not see Riley unless she had a hair follicle test that was drug-free. A drug-free hair follicle test would mean she could not use any substances for at least 90 days, and that didn't happen. In the divorce, Elizabeth was given a specific time, 6:00pm to 8:00pm each day, when she could call and talk to Riley. She wasn't allowed to tell him that she was his mother.

February 11, 2009 Superior Court of New Jersey, Criminal Division

Elizabeth is officially admitted into:
State of New Jersey Drug Court Program.

Conditions of Drug Court:
- To appear at Drug Court weekly on Wednesdays in Courtroom D at 8:30am
- To submit to random urine monitoring
- To attend five 12-step meetings per week; if employed, three meetings per week
- To remain arrest free
- To remain alcohol and drug free, participate in IOP (Intensive Out Patient)

Pines Hospitalization

February 13, 2009: Emergency Department to Pines

Elizabeth was depressed after seeing Riley for just a day and then having to leave him again. She told me she wanted to die. She said she was pissed off at two friends because they woke her up when she was turning blue/overdosing. Elizabeth had told her friends to toss her out on the street if she was overdosing because she wanted to die. She agreed I could take her to the emergency department to be evaluated.

At the emergency department, the concerned attitude of the nurses abruptly changed and became cold and uncaring when Elizabeth told them she had heroin, crack, and marijuana in her system. After she waited almost 24 hours to be seen, the psychiatrist determined she was suicidal due to separation from her baby. She agreed to go to the Pines voluntarily.

February 15, 2009: Elizabeth's Private Journal at Pines

Day two in the psych ward. As many times as I've thought I belonged in one, now I'm pretty sure I don't. I thought I was here voluntarily but now I learn I'm "conditional voluntary," which means if I don't participate in groups or if I sleep during the day (which I feel like I need to because I'm kicking heroin), they can put me on "involuntary" and I could be here for months.

They put me on Celexa, an SSRI, which can increase thoughts of suicide, especially if you have a history of bipolar disorder (my mom) in your family. I don't think a pill will fix the pain I feel from being away from my Riley. He's my heart and I don't know if I can live clear headed and drug free w/out my favorite boy.

February 16, 2009: Elizabeth's Private Journal at Pines

I want to fucking scream. My stomach is killing me.
♫ "In the Pines, in the Pines, where the sun don't ever shine, I'll shiver the whole night through." [Nirvana lyrics]

Worksheet Completed Today
1.   I abuse: heroin/cocaine/alcohol/marijuana
2.   I have: depression and anxiety/panic attacks
3.   I came to the hospital because: my mom thought I was a danger to myself
4.   The reasons I want to change my drug/alcohol habits are: to get my son back & be happy/ joyous/free & make something of myself
5.   The steps I plan to take to change my drug/alcohol habits are: go to IOP or partial hospitalization
6.   The things that will prevent me from changing are: ANGER, insecurity
7.   The strengths I possess that can help me change are: empathy, intelligence

February 17, 2009: Elizabeth's Private Journal at Pines

I'm feeling better today. I dreamed about Riley. As long as I go to IOP or whatever they suggest I should be able to eventually get more custody. I just talked to Bobby and my mom & I feel great, probably because of this wonderful drug called Celexa... I've decided to use the loss of my baby to fuel my fight against my disease. My name is

Elizabeth, I'm a drug/money/sex/everything addict and now I'm certifiable.

My Mitigating Factors
sexual abuse
Riley
completed high school w/ 1400 SATs
scholarship to college; flunked out due to anxiety
Dad is not supportive, doesn't believe in MICA
rape
PTSD
bipolar mother

February 18, 2009: Elizabeth's Private Journal at Pines

I had a good night. I talked a lot about Riley and showed off my pictures of him. Someone said he was so beautiful he should be a baby model. I've always thought of him as the most amazing creature I've ever seen.

February 19, 2009: Elizabeth's Private Journal at Pines

I'm leaving this loony bin. I woke up this morning to my whacked out roommate Maude screaming bc they had to give her a shot of Haldol. Now there's someone yelling about God knows what, and a third is singing. I can't wait to see my Riley again. I know I don't belong here. I know what I have to do to get him back in my life. Right now I'm laughing inside while in "Anxiety Group" w/Pam bc Mitch told me earlier he wanted to know what her underwear looked like.

Jail

February 20, 2009: County Courthouse/Jail

Elizabeth had a meeting with her drug court probation officer. She admitted to him she had used crack and heroin before she went into the hospital. She was taken to the county jail.

March 3, 2009: Letter from County Jail

Hey Ma,

Yesterday we had another shakedown. I admitted I had some cigarette roaches & so far (keep your fingers crossed) I didn't get charged. I'm hoping they appreciated my honesty. I can't wait to see you tomorrow. I love you so much and I miss you. I wish there was something I could do for you. I know it's hard & I want you to know that I know how you feel. I wish I could take it away. I'm sending you a picture w/ quotes I picked out from a poetry book. Enjoy. . I can't wait to get out and get tattoos and get tan and I'm gonna make you get a pedicure. Sound good?

I miss you so much Mama! I love you more than anything (except Riley).

Love you, Miss you, Mean it, Little Lizzie

PS I enclosed a letter for DJ. Please send him the pic of me & him or just a hot pic of me.

Thank you. (Please don't read it). I'm serious, you'll get grossed out!!!

March 6, 2009: Letter from County Jail

It's Friday night & I'm in a very good mood because you just told me that you bought me that adorable dress I've had my eye on. I'll wear it with my brown boots or something equally cute! Thanks for making me smile, you have no idea how much I appreciate it. Commissary comes tomorrow. I'll have sweatpants, shampoo & conditioner, Dove soap (hopefully it will clear up my face), coffee, hot cocoa, soup, peanut butter, jelly, popcorn, & some sweets. You have no idea how depressing it is to be in here w/out $$. It makes you feel like no one cares. Plus this food doesn't make you full. You eat dinner and you're hungry by 7pm, starved by the time breakfast comes. I've been waking up @ 5:30am bc I'm so famished & breakfast doesn't come until six. I will be so happy to see you tomorrow. I almost forgot Dad's coming too. I'm praying for a smooth visit.

March 7, 2009: Letter from County Jail

Mom, It's Saturday morning. You just came to visit me like an hour ago and I guess I'm relieved that Daddy didn't show. It's a beautiful winter wonderland – wish I was going out in the woods w/ [dog] like I used to do. Some of my fondest memories. I was at peace with a canine best friend (usually smoking weed). I miss you and I look forward to cooking for you and participating in lots of other wholesome activities in order to maintain my sobriety when I get out. That's not just lip service, it's a true desire. Ooh "Face-Off" just came on. Sexy Nic Cage. I really think this Celexa is working, now if only I could find something for my anxiety. I'll just have to practice relaxation techniques, etc. until I'm off Drug Court.

I really need to get to the dentist. My 4 cavities from 2 years ago are killing me and who knows, w/ the ghetto toothpaste they give us here, since I've spent over 5 months in jail this past year, I probably have more cavities now. I keep fantasizing about taking Riley to Disney World, maybe for his 2nd birthday. Wouldn't that be the greatest? Hey, I can dream, can't I. To get by in here, I think you really need to live in a fantasy world or else you'd drive yourself crazy.

March 8, 2009: Letter from County Jail

Hey Mama!

I wanted to apologize for the way I've been acting, especially in the visit last night. I know sorry doesn't take back anything I said. I'm so frustrated. K. from Drug Court came to see me. She said I'll most likely be sent to Straight & Narrow [locked rehab] for 18 months. Just so you know, the whole 18 months in Straight & Narrow does not count towards my 5 years of Drug Court. I'm so frustrated so I'll stop writing about that. I got letters from Eddie & DJ & Sam today. I also got my books today!! Thank you sooooo much! The yoga book is awesome & the novel looks good. Thank you for brightening my day mama. I miss you! I love you! Sorry I've been so angry & negative. Thank you for being there for me.

Love, Elizabeth

March 10, 2009: Letter from County Jail

Mom,

We just watched "House" & the end song was Ben Harper's "Waiting on an Angel". I forgot how much I am completely in love with his music, how much it touches me & how twice now his music has brought me out of my addiction. Have I ever told you about that? I was living @

89

Bob's & had been smoking crack & Kristin picked me up & we went to the Electric Factory to see Ben Harper. I felt awful but as soon as I heard him, I had a spiritual awakening – he sang "Faded" and it was amazing. Then when Axel & I were in Mexico, we were tripping on acid & I said I wanted to hear Ben Harper & the college kids had a mix CD & "Susie Blue" started playing. I forgot to tell you, they TURNED OFF THE CABLE in here. We only get up to channel 22, everyone is so pissed. That means no movies on weekends.

I love you & miss you &
I'm not going to mistreat you
or direct my frustrations @ you anymore
because all you've done is try to help me

Love, Little Lizzie

March 11, 2009 Letter from County Jail

!Hola Mamacita!

I know I've been downright mean lately & sorry doesn't really help anything. I've been misdirecting my anger & frustrations at you because you are the only person I have to talk to. It's no excuse and the only way I can make it up to you is not by saying I'm sorry, but working on my self-control & anger. I need to stop trying to make other people hurt just because I do. I'm asking Jean C for another copy of the Anger Management Packet and this time, I will finish it. I did not mean the awful things I said. I am grateful for you & have the most respect for what you've done as a parent.

I've been doing a lot of soul searching & journaling. I've also been going to meetings & church & I want to let go of the bitterness I carry because it is an ugly quality & I want to become the best version of myself. I hope that someday soon I'll make you proud & make it worth all the love & time & patience etc. you've invested in me. Please forgive me & my misguided rage. It doesn't have anything to do with you. Thank you for helping me to believe that I was meant for greater things & that despite my past I can rise above & be a wonderful mom & exceptional person. Please don't give up on me, Mommy. I know I can do this if I stay busy, go to meetings, find a sponsor, work the steps, & not be afraid to ask for help. I fully intend to do that, unless I want to die all alone.

Love, Elizabeth

Elizabeth's <u>Anger Management Packet</u> March 13, 2009: County Jail

Who looked after you and raised you?
- My mother, most of the time
- My father, maybe 2 days a week & from 4-10 years old his gf K and from 11-18 my stepmom

Describe the people who looked after you.
- My mother is bipolar and half the time she had an overabundance of energy and she would do crazy stuff, go to bars…The other half she would be in bed for days and cry all the time
- My dad was fun but very critical, nothing I did was ever good enough even though I was an exceptional child. I was afraid of disappointing him

How did they get along with you?
- My mom was proud of me but got irritated when I refused to clean my room
- I did lots of fun activities w/ my dad but he yelled @ me a lot

91

Did they spend a lot of time playing with you?
- My dad took me to a lot of interesting places but he ignored me when he was working even though we only had a little time together. Sometimes I wouldn't hear from him for a week
- My mom spent a lot of time, she paid attention except when she was depressed

What happened when you did something wrong as a child? (Did someone scold you, ground you, spank you or hit you? Were you punished in some other way)?
- My mother said she was disappointed in me or grounded me when I got older
- My dad yelled

Did you think your family was different from everyone else's family at the time?
- Yes, everyone else had two parents in their house, my mom was "crazy," & I had half-siblings. I wanted my mom to be more strict but she felt bad bc my father was so hard on me

Looking back, how was your family different from or the same as other families?
- Now I know more people who come from broken homes, other people have mental illness in their families

Did the people who looked after you ever have run-ins with the law?
- No, never

Do you think you are serving time now because of the way you were treated as a child?

- I think that my addiction is a result of a genetic predisposition & my perception of how I was treated, my lack of self-esteem/self-confidence, & the shame of sexual abuse

How did the people who looked after you punish other members of your family?(brothers or sisters)
- I hardly ever saw my ½ siblings

How did the people who looked after you punish each other?
- My dad called my mom names & yelled @ her

Did anyone ever abuse you physically or sexually as a child?
- Yes

If so, describe how you felt.
- I felt very ashamed afterward but it was a pleasurable physical feeling. I think mentally, it made me confuse sex with love & is why I have been labeled a "sex addict"

How do you feel about being hurt in the past?
- I feel like it was my fault

Looking back, do you think the members of your family truly cared for you?
- Yes, my dad was hard on me because he wanted me to live up to my potential
- My mother definitely cared

Describe your close friends when you were young.

- My best friend Lauren was the minister's daughter. She was honest, intelligent, kind & silly. I went to her house a lot after school

Kicked Out of Drug Court

March 18, 2009: County Court

Elizabeth is kicked out of drug court because of her psych hospitalization and history of mental health issues.

March 29, 2009: Letter from County Jail

Hi Mommy!

I've been dreaming about Riley a lot. Won't it be great when we can take him to Disney World? I can't wait! I know in my other letters I've asked questions or requested reading material. Can you please respond to my previous inquiries – "I would be much obliged," (said in lovely British accent)... Ooh, have you smelled Estee Lauder 'Sensuous'? It's tres magnifique! (My friend gets *Instyle* magazine sent to her in here.) I'll see you tomorrow night at visit.

Thanks for coming to visit. I always get mad at myself for taking out my frustrations on you when you visit. I just want to tell you that your visits & the sugar cookies we get are all I look forward to in here & you make me smile for hours after the visit. Thank you for making me feel loved Mommy! I showed off my pictures of Riley today. I miss him so. This morning somebody turned on the show "Calliou". Did I ever tell you how I sang the theme song & substituted Riley's name for Calliou? It made me smile but sad at the same time. I miss you & I can't wait to get out & exercise w/you & cook & go tanning. Sound good?

Love, Little Lizzie

Probation

Elizabeth has a court date. The judge chose to sentence her to probation rather than prison. The judge:

> "At age 24, Defendant has convictions for more than 3 municipal court offenses. Ms. _____ was enrolled in the Pretrial Intervention Program on two indictments in 2005. She was granted an extension in Pretrial Intervention for 12 months in May 2008. She was terminated in June 2008. She admits using alcohol, marijuana, cocaine, and heroin. Defendant is an addict who will remain lawless until the addiction is dealt with effectively. Defendant has certain mental health issues which include serious anxiety, serious depression, bi-polar, cutting herself, suicidal ideation, and overdosing. Given their quality and nature, the mitigating factors preponderate over the aggravating factors. This defendant truly needs substance abuse treatment and mental health treatment. This negotiated plea agreement appears fair to the state as well as the defendant, and in the interest of justice the recommended sentence will be imposed."

Elizabeth is sentenced to 5 years of probation and released from jail.

April 10, 2009

A friend let Elizabeth stay in an empty apartment. She had a probation drug test that was positive for marijuana and cocaine.

April 19, 2009

Elizabeth admitted to her probation officer that she had used Controlled Dangerous Substance(s).

April 20, 2009

Elizabeth had a probation drug test that was positive for marijuana, opiates, and cocaine.

Elizabeth's Voicemail to Sheila April 21st, 2009, 10:41pm

"Hey mommy, I just wanted to let you know that, um, K and I have decided on our own that we need to stop seeing each other, you know, we're making a mature decision to just be friends, because we realize that we're not good for each other's sobriety and, um also, she gave me back my wallet, so there! and I'll always love her. Have sweet dreams I love you bye."

Violation of Probation, Jail, and Support for Elizabeth

April 22, 2009: County Jail

Elizabeth is arrested for violation of probation and taken to the county jail.

April 22, 2009: Letter (unsent) from Elizabeth to Judge S re: Probation Violation

Dear Honorable Judge S:

I, Elizabeth _____, am writing you today with sincere apology at being before you again so soon. I'm not trying to make excuses for my regrettable behavior, but I would like to explain to you the events that have transpired within the past thirty days.

Upon my release, I had full intentions and a strong desire to live a drug free life. For the first few days, I attended nightly 12-step meetings. Despite the fact that I would not be able to see my son, Riley on Easter, I was looking forward to seeing my extended family for our traditional Easter dinner. Due in part to my previous relapse, my family was still upset with me and I was not invited. I was saddened and lonely on this day that I could not be with my family. I decided to go to a meeting. On the way to the meeting, I encountered three acquaintances from my past. The third of which was someone I had previously had a relationship with but tried to avoid because they are not clean and sober. I let my emotions cloud my judgment, and decided to go with her. Hindsight is 20/20, I can see now the mistakes I made that led up to my relapse and eventually landed me back in that orange jumpsuit. I should have used my support network for help: my probation officer, my mother, my fellow recovering addicts.

Violation of Probation – April 24, 2009: Summary

Probation Adjustment: Poor. Ms. _____ already failed Pretrial Intervention and had spent 46 days in County Jail prior to being sentenced 4/08/09. She obviously started using almost immediately upon her release. A warrant was issued 4/21/09 and executed 4/22/09.

Recommendation: To remain incarcerated **until accepted into long term inpatient facility**. Probation has a serious concern regarding whether or not this defendant can remain clean and sober at all, even after completion of any inpatient program.

April 24, 2009: Letter from County Jail

Hey Mama!

I miss you so much & I hope you know how much I love and appreciate you. You have no idea how depressing it is to be back in here. Even the other inmates look at me like I'm a loser, not to mention the officers & nurses. They won't give me any detox meds so I feel like shit. Oh & I have no feeling in my hands. I don't know what's wrong with me. I'm just laying here freezing, imagining us laying in the Florida sun.

Now it's **Sunday** & I still don't have feeling in my hands. This morning the guard asked me what I was doing back & he outright called me stupid. It also doesn't help that I'm not getting my Celexa. I wish I could talk to you. My soul aches, that's the only way I can explain how I feel. Maybe when my meds come in I'll feel better. Could you please send me some pictures. Maybe since Axel wants you in Riley's life he'll send some recent photos.

Hey Ma, it's now **Monday** night. I was looking forward to your visit but now it's come and gone and I feel worse. I know you're worried about me but I was expecting to see your smiling face. You asked me what has changed. What I didn't tell you about my last 2 weeks out there was that 2 – no 3 guys made me break down and cry – one was Hank, who made me feel like a piece of shit in front of his roommates & then Mike, who thought I just wanted him for his money & made me cry hysterically. Then my one dealer 'E' walked in, took a look at me, said "I don't even want to see you" (because of the dope & I looked like shit). He was supposed to give me drugs for fucking him but he said he was fed up.

Which reminds me, one drug dealer doesn't sell to me anymore, because he refuses to fuel my addiction any longer. It pretty much boils down to the fact that I don't want to give up Riley and I don't want to end up some career junkie. If even my dealers don't want to see me doing what I was doing, I know I don't belong in that world. When I fantasize in here, it has nothing to do with drugs. It's about family, people I care about, music, art, sun, food, things that I enjoy when I'm sober & that I ignore when I'm not. This is the Emancipation of Lizzie and I'm ready to reclaim my place in society as a contributing mother, daughter, sister, worker.

Love, Elizabeth

May 2009: Letters in Support of Elizabeth Sent to Judge S

We knew that because of her violation of probation, Elizabeth would be sentenced to state prison. Drug court terminated her (after formally admitting her) due to her mental health history. They had told Elizabeth they were going to send her to Straight & Narrow, a locked rehab, for 18 months.

When Elizabeth violated probation, her probation officer recommended she remain incarcerated until accepted into a long-term inpatient facility. I decided to appeal to Elizabeth's judge – to send her to long term rehab and not prison. I reasoned that since drug court had planned to send her to Straight & Narrow for 18 months, and since her probation officer had officially recommended a long-term inpatient facility, maybe Judge S would follow the drug court evaluator's recommendation and the probation officer's recommendation. They had both agreed that Elizabeth needed long term rehab. I wrote a petition describing Elizabeth's situation, I made copies and I distributed them to Elizabeth's family, friends, and teachers. More than 40 people wrote to the judge on Elizabeth's behalf requesting she be sent to long term rehab not prison.

RD – I was Elizabeth's kindergarten teacher. I remember her as a kind, quick class member who loved learning new skills, singing songs, and drawing pictures about animals and other things in nature. Please give her the opportunity to benefit from rehab, not prison. I know she has the potential to give back to society when she is well.

KS – I was Elizabeth's Sunday School teacher and Girl Scout leader. She was my daughter's best friend. She was a bright, beautiful girl who would benefit from rehab – not prison. She needs intensive substance & mental health treatment, so she can return to whom she was – a talented, loving girl with much to offer to our society.

DM – I taught Elizabeth in Elementary School and also advised her as her spelling coach. She was our school's 1999 spelling champion and she was runner-up at the county level. She was a gentle soul and a highly intelligent and talented young lady. Her forte was literature and written language. Life's events have led her down a long and dangerous path, but I believe that Liz has the potential to be a productive and contributing citizen. Please give her a chance to reach her potential and to use her intelligence for productive purposes. Thank you.

KA – Dear Judge S, I dearly love my niece, Elizabeth, and am saddened by the trouble she is now having. I feel she needs long term medical help, not prison, as she is not a criminal, just a very troubled young woman.

JP (Elizabeth's Uncle) – I have known Liz since birth. She was always a bright, caring, and loving child growing up. All through school she had perfect grades and loved learning. Our family thought she would go so far in life. We just did not know it would be this far down. Drug Addiction has taken the girl we all know and love and turned her into someone we barely know. We feel that long term rehab will give her a second chance at life.

103

Please give her this chance to come back to us so we don't lose her forever. Thank you for your consideration.

BN – Elizabeth is my niece and I have known her since she was a small child. I have not seen her in recent years, but we have had extensive telephone conversations when she reached out for help with her addictions. I know Elizabeth to be a kind and loving spirit who has an extreme self-destructive addictive personality and illness. A long term residential rehab combined with a halfway house would provide the best possible outcome. I humbly ask you to do a most generous act and sentence Elizabeth to Long Term Residential Rehab. It will take a leap of faith to trust in her, but she is a worthy human being. I pray you will not be disappointed, Judge S.

DN – I am Elizabeth's uncle. I believe prison is a place for criminals, not a place for people with a disease. Elizabeth needs long term rehab to have any chance to survive and become the person she can be. Please consider your sentence with this in mind. Thank you.

LS – I have known Elizabeth for 19 years. She was my best friend growing up, and I care about her deeply. Liz is a kind and intelligent woman. She was my confidant and closest friend during my tough preteen/teen years. Although Elizabeth has struggled in these past few years, I know that she is destined to get back on track, and make this world a better place. With some help, through long term rehabilitation, I know that she will be able to show the qualities that made her my very best friend.

May 13, 2009: Letter from County Jail

Hola Mamacita,

It's another dreary day so we haven't been out for yard. I read all of the support "petitions" to Judge S, and although it was depressing knowing that all those people know how far down the scale I've gone, it was uplifting to see that they believe that I can still live up to my potential.

Colleen was kind enough to share a cinnamon roll from commissary w/ me – the highlight of my day. Mmm…jailhouse Cinnabon. We put the package in the hot water to warm it up, clever huh?

I'm sorry if I was frustrated while talking to you at our visit, but thank you for listening. I did feel a whole lot better after seeing you Ma. Thank you for loving me enough to try to save me from myself. I realize how out of control I was. I don't have fun anymore out there. I'm ready to surrender myself & let go of all my baggage. I hope I get a good therapist because I'm ready to unload all this shit I've been carrying around. Sorry to cut this short but they're calling for mail & my hand hurts. I love you, I miss you, I mean it!

Love, Little Lizzie

May 15, 2009 Elizabeth's Missing Drugs/Not Missing Drugs Worksheet (Jail)

I Will Miss…
1. Excitement of getting drug
2. The way it makes me feel (or not feel)
3. Being in control of what I feel
4. Feeling like I have no responsibilities
5. Thrill of being bad
6. Not caring about anything

7. Loss of anxiety
8. People that understand me
9. Getting **skinny**

I Will Not Miss…
1. Consequences: jail, rehab, probation
2. Strained family relationships
3. Not having $ for other things
4. How it feels to run out
5. Disrespecting myself

May 25, 2009: Letter from County Jail

Hey Mom,

I just got your long letter & it was much appreciated. I started to write this letter a while ago but haven't really been in a writing mood. About the alcohol, [Elizabeth, or her dorm, was caught w/ alcohol] I took the blame, it wasn't just mine – I said no one else knew about it so that no one else would get in trouble. People were going up to state prison & were afraid the charge would follow them. That's all the time I want to spend on that subject.

I wanted to know if you could do me a favor & send Donna (in here too) a card & a perfume sample. She's sad cuz she doesn't get a lot of mail. Thanks Mom! I'm sooo excited for our road trip! [Furlough to visit rehab] I can't wait for Mickey D's for breakfast and to sing to the radio w/ you!! I miss you! I've started reading *The Lovely Bones* & I can't put it down! It's sooo good! Thanks for getting everything set for me to go see the rehab. I am starting to get excited to change my life & focus on myself. No guys to get in the way, etc.

Love you, Miss you, Mean it! Little Lizzie

May 31, 2009: County Jail

Dearest Mother,

I thought I'd write you a letter this evening since it's been a while since my last correspondence. We're lucky this afternoon – "Scrubs" is on TV instead of the steady stream of crap shows we're forced to watch hour after hour, day after day. "Scrubs" reminds me of being with you in Moab. Despite the craziness, we did have some fun times…I would bring back pizza from work for you; you & I would go to the frozen yogurt/coffee drive-through coffee booth where Jon's [Moab boyfriend] brother Sasha worked & I collected the stickers. Hmmm, maybe I should be a dietician/nutritionist; do you see how all these memories relate to food?

I cannot wait for June 9th [Furlough from jail for me to take Elizabeth to visit a Christian rehab]. I hope I like the place. You know what I'd like to read at rehab? *Clapton* by Eric Clapton. Thank you soooo much for buying me those dresses. That was very sweet of you. Thanks for being the best mommy ever! I can't wait until we can listen to music together! Maybe I won't have a hissy fit if you sing.

Donna & I have a wall (we're in a corner of the room & share the wall space) of beauty in which we plaster the cinder blocks w/ pictures: Riley, the beach, Live Your Best Life Calendar, Adam Lambert & Chris Allen, David Beckham, Jordana Brewster, Zac Efron, Bar Refaeli, Lindsay Lohan & Chace Crawford. The others call it our lesbian wall because there are gorgeous girls in various stages of undress. Well I'll see you at visit tomorrow. I love you Ma!

Little Lizzie

June 9, 2009: Furlough to visit rehab, back to County Jail

Judge S approved our request for a furlough in order to visit The Good News Home for Women rehab. I picked Elizabeth up at the jail and drove her for a tour and interview at the Christian rehab. Elizabeth and I immediately got a weird vibe. Very quickly we knew that this rehab was not suitable. It was too restrictive, too focused on bible study. Elizabeth felt she would not feel safe in an inpatient rehab that had no psychiatric care. She believed she would probably run. Elizabeth would be a fugitive if she ran away. So it was back to jail.

June 18, 2009: Letter from County Jail

Hola Mamacita!

How are you doing? Well I was extremely happy to hear about your courageous appearance at that party. It's an inspiration to me when you overcome your 'perceived limitations' and step out of your comfort zone and enjoy yourself. It shows me that anything is possible and it's never too late to change.

Guess what? Rachel left 3 hours ago to go to rehab but they made her come back after they gave her a psych evaluation. Oh, I saw [school friend] in processing. He acted like he didn't see me.

I want to thank you for the time we got to spend together on my furlough. I had a blast in the car ride singing & talking with you. Well I'll see you tomorrow. Thanks for being you.

Love, your best daughter, Little Lizzie

New Jersey State Prison

July 9, 2009: County Court

We never heard from Judge S. I don't know if she read the letters in support of Elizabeth. Elizabeth was sentenced to three years in New Jersey State Prison (Edna Mahan Correctional Facility for Women) for possession of controlled dangerous substance, three years for conspiracy to possess one Klonopin pill, and 18 months for attempted shoplifting, to be served concurrently.

July 2009: Elizabeth's Unsent Letter from County Jail

Dear Family and Friends,

Thank you for showing your support. I greatly appreciate your taking the time to write Judge S on my behalf. Regretfully, I accepted a plea bargain of 3 years in Edna Mahan Correctional Facility in Clinton. Unfortunately, we were unable to find an adequate rehab. I am continuing to work on my recovery, with the ultimate goal of being reunited with my son, Riley.

Thanks again! Sincerely, Elizabeth

July 24, 2009: County Jail Transfer to Edna Mahan Correctional Facility

Mama,

Well I know you can't wait to hear about my excellent adventure so I will give a play by play of my thrilling exodus from the greatly accommodating, always warm and hospitable… good ol' County Jail. I'm sure when you called this morning to make the appointment to visit they informed you that I was now STATE PROPERTY!

So it all started out as any other normal Thursday morning. I ate my breakfast, smoked a cigarette, went back to sleep, and politely declined meds. I go back to dreamland and awaken to the sweet voices of TRAYS!! I get my lunch… all I eat is the brownie & carrots. I smoke an after lunch cig, and leisurely make my first cup of Joe. As I am about to take the first delicious sip of my perfectly blended McCafe substitute, I am distracted by a guard at the gate, he says "Smith, ROLL UP, Jones, ROLL UP, [Elizabeth], ROLL UP!

WHAATT?!? Oh no he's got to be kidding me. I wasn't ready for this. Agh. I only have about 5 minutes to pack my shit. I said my goodbyes and got searched by DOC [Department of Corrections]. We drove shackled in a van for over 2 hrs. to wait at St. Francis Hospital in Trenton until a different driver came to get us. We sat for hours until the guard came to put our handcuffs back on. I had to go to the bathroom so she yelled at me for holding her up. Then we walk out the door, and she says "do you have any property?" We say "yeah, right there." She says "go get it." So I reach for it & she screams "don't ever walk behind me, bitch!" Then it's another hr. til we get there. We go to the Max [maximum security] hospital for 4 hrs. Then they finally send us to the prison reception area.

So, prison reception. Yes, the food in the Max mess hall is worse than County Jail. We do our cleaning jobs, sign up for yard & wait to go out, where if we're lucky, we can smoke. I played "pig" today w/a deflated basketball. One guard sits in a tower, another drives around the whole Max unit. Then we come in, lunch, then I read & write, and usually take a nap. I get up around 3:30pm, read some more, then play Scrabble or talk or watch whatever in-house movie they have on for a 12 hr period. Lights out, no talking after 11pm. I should be in reception for at least 2 or 3 weeks. Then Max for a week, then grounds.

I'm jailin' mama. Everything happens for a reason: I go to the bookshelf and the first one I pick up is *White Oleander*, which I just left 150 pages unfinished in County, and *My Darling, My Hamburger* by Paul Zindel, which I feel was written for me!! I really need some music in my life, can you send lyrics to the Fray, "I found God," Pearl Jam "I Got ID" etc.

Love, Lizabuf

July 25, 2009: Edna Mahan Correctional Facility for Women, New Jersey Department of Corrections

Elizabeth's Medical and Psychiatric Summary

- Hepatitis C
- Cocaine Abuse in Institutional Remission
- Opioid Abuse in Institutional Remission
- Opioid-Induced Mood Disorder
- Depressive Disorder NOS
- Risk of Suicide & Self Inflicted Injury
- Risk of Self-Mutilation
- Amphetamine Abuse
- Panic Disorder with Agoraphobia
- Other (or Unknown) Substance Abuse
- Smoker

July 25, 2009: Letter from Edna Mahan Correctional Facility

Alright Ma, this is how it goes down in here:
Everyone has got a hustle, a way of surviving. I just put in my order for emergency commissary. If I could get some smokes from Pinky (who told me she'd take care of me when I got up here) I would be fine. I'm going to need $$ (at least $150 for prescriptions, repaying emergency commissary, getting my teeth fixed, a t shirt, toothpaste, shampoo, deodorant, a toothbrush, a real razor, soap, lotion, envelopes, stamps, cigs, coffee, and a few snack items) (believe me I don't pig out like I used to, by the time you see me I'll probably have lost 15 pounds!). Hopefully that will keep me set for my entire stay at the luxurious Hotel Edna Mahan. I'll need it ASAP, not trying to be greedy/spoiled but if I don't order commissary in a week, I'm screwed!

Love, Lizzie

July 26, 2009: Letter from Edna Mahan Correctional Facility

Hey Ma!

There is a god! I just got my pics, bible etc. that I'm allowed to keep & your letters from July 17th & 18th that had arrived in County Jail the day I left but were unopened. They made me so happy! I don't know what I'd do without your words in this prison. And yes Mommy, I'm still here, I'm still your Little Lizabuf. I want to take this time to expand my mind, vocabulary, writing and art skills, find my passion. People here don't talk about drugs like in the County.

112

I saw the psychiatrist. He put me on Celexa [antidepressant], Lamictal [mood stabilizer], and Klonopin! [anxiety]. I feel like a normal human being again. If I could only have a smoke…

It's hard when you're in this place to think yourself in a positive way. You're treated like the scum of the earth. Except for a few (like Killah, who murdered her kids' father), most people in here are just drug addicts who have made some wrong choices. I try to make the most of this time here by reading and practicing yoga. I try to envision a happier time that's yet to come. I can't wait until you, me, & Riley are in Disney World together. I miss you & I'm sorry I don't have much to write about. You really brightened my week, Mommy.

Love &Hugs, Your Little Lizzie

July 26, 2009: Letter from Edna Mahan Correctional Facility

Dear Gram & Pop-pop,

I regret not writing to you sooner. How do I explain my deplorable acts, my guilt, my shame, and just the complete and utter mess my life has become? Especially to two of the most supportive, caring, loving people who have invested so much time, energy, support, money, and love into someone who has proven time and time again unworthy and undeserving of all these blessings. All I can do now is ask for your forgiveness in the hopes that one day, God willing, I will be worthy, a good mother, daughter, granddaughter, friend, employee, creator, etc. I know it's going to be a long road ahead and I need to be honest, open minded, and willing. I hope and believe that I can be reborn into the "sweet, intelligent girl" that I was "prior to drugs." I love you Grammy, I love you Pop-pop. I miss you both more than you know.

Love, Elizabeth
PS Enclosed in the envelope are a big hug and an even bigger smile.

July 27, 2009: Letter from Edna Mahan Correctional Facility

Time: 10:30 am
Song: Gloomy Sunday, Artist: Sarah McLachlan
Mood: depressed, singled out, alone

Dear Best Mommy in the world,

This is when it started: I asked Officer D (the most miserable bitch who hates those who are prettier than her) if I could practice my yoga in the public area. She said "no, do it on your bed." So I did. She watched me. I read a little, and then it was dinner time. When we got back from dinner, she calls me over and tells me she found a cig under my mattress. I said it was mine and she told me I was getting 5 days Loss of Recreation Privileges [LORP]. (That means no yard, no sitting in the public area, no watching TV, I have to stay on my bunk except for meals, meds, showers, and 20 minutes to use the phone). So then she says, "If you are so worried about yoga, then why are you smoking?"

She asks if I'd like to talk to the sergeant about it. I didn't know what to do except say yes, hoping he'd be reasonable & maybe let me just work extra hours instead. He was an asshole about it & said I was lucky I didn't get a blue sheet (<u>very bad,</u> can hurt my parole chances). I learn I can watch "Bachelorette" since my punishment doesn't start until tomorrow. She makes me mop the hallway even

114

though it's not my job. All of a sudden I hear a few of the others talking about how I'm tearing up magazines (I'm making a collage for you), pretty much snitching on me (which they claim all the time, "Snitches get stitches & thrown into ditches.")

Then the fuckin' cop says, "Don't worry I'll take care of that." Then I'm mopping, and when I finish up, I'm on the verge of tears. At least I get to watch the last few emotional minutes of "Bachelorette" so I can mask the reason why I'm really crying. Then I get in my bed and finally the lights go out so I can have a much needed cig. (I traded my boots for someone else's & 3 cigs) <u>Don't ever write back about anything incriminating.</u>

At this moment I hate my life, myself, my weakness, my abandoning my son. I just want so badly to curl up with you and Riley and watch a movie. That's how it should have been but I fucked everything up. How will I ever get him back? And if I ever see him again, he won't know me from some fuckin' skank Axel brings home. I am disgusting, worthless, the list goes on and on. So now I have to worry about how this guard is gonna "take care of me." I swear to God, Mom, I won't hesitate to whoop someone's ass just because she deserves it and I know I have enough hatred in me to take all my rage out on someone & snatch the life right out of them.

Ok. I need to change gears. I am not defined by my labels: criminal, deadbeat mom, college dropout. I am intelligent, caring, creative, humorous, artistic, gifted, compassionate, empathetic – just trying to find my path in life. I'm adventurous, I love to travel, write (now that I'm on Klonopin again, I long to put all my thoughts on paper). I want to paint, draw, practice & hone my artistic talents. I miss you so much. I just want to be with my mommy. I need you. "Like water, like breath, like rain, I need you like mercy from heaven's gate". (LeAnn Rimes)

Please don't leave me again [referring to when she stayed with her dad for her senior year of high school and I moved out west]. I want you to have your own life but I need you to help me figure everything out (this terrible, disastrous mess I've made of my life). I want my Baby and I need to see him soon or I don't really see the point in anything anymore. Oh well, I just remembered your words of wisdom Mama: "Everything seems better in the morning." Goodnight, I love you. I'm the luckiest daughter in the world to have you. I just wish my son will be able to say the same about me. 'Night, I wish you were here to sing "Edelweiss" to me.

Love, Lizzie

July 30, 2009: Letter from Edna Mahan Correctional Facility

Song: I'm With You, Artist: Avril Lavigne
Mood: hopeful, poetic, creative, singled out, longing just to hear Riley speak

Ma. I've had a lot to deal with bc of my infraction. A certain officer has taken an extreme dislike to me & recruited other female cops to do some singling out on me too.

Parole came to see me & my PED [parole eligibility date] is 9/14/09.

I understand why you told me about Axel [living w/ girlfriend]. I wrote a letter that I'm enclosing & am trusting you to email to him VERBATIM, & keep the paper copy for my records **so I can include it in my book**. Please send it ASAP. I need closure. I do want pics of me & Axel so I can symbolically burn them, and show my ex to my friends. I miss you. I didn't get a letter today, hopefully tomorrow. Here's to new beginnings. I'm off LORP [restrictions] on

Sunday, praise the Lord. Please ask my Daddy to take the block off his phone. Two other girls from the County just got here!

Love you, Miss you, Mean it! Little Lizzie

July 30, 2009: Elizabeth's above-mentioned letter to Axel

Axel,

If it has not been made clear to you, since the year I've been back in NJ, I've been living a hell of my own design. Life without you, Riley and the kids [her step-kids, Axel's kids] holds no meaning. Riley is my heart, my soul, my home, my baby, my love. When I'm with Riley, I feel such joy, amazement, and pride. Without my little bunny I am homeless, heartbroken, my soul aches. I retreat into what I know. A downward spiral sucks me into a pit of despair. The snakes coil around my neck and I acquiesce into their underworld.

Axel, we've been through hell and hurricanes together. We both made unforgivable and unforgotten mistakes against each other. I want nothing more than to have a civil, friendly, cooperative and compromising relationship in order to give our son the best chance to have a blessed, healthy, happy, fulfilling, and love-filled life.

Please tuck my son in at night and tell him his mommy loves him – he's her little bunny, her angel. I will get a phone card so that I can call to speak to Riley at my court-directed nightly time. I appreciate your cooperation in this custody issue.

PS If anything, you taught me how to be a stronger woman – that what does not kill you only makes you

117

stronger. Yes I am a liar, yes I am a sinner, please forgive my broken soul. They made this world so hard.

August 1, 2009: Letter from Edna Mahan Correctional Facility

Song: Since U Been Gone, Artist: Kelly Clarkson
Mood: enlightened, in solitude, centered & focused

Well mother, I hope you said "Rabbit, Rabbit" this glorious morn! I wrote it on my right hand & tied a string around my left pointer finger so that I would remember. As soon as I woke up, I said it & have been having a good day (as good as you can have in prison, anyway) ever since. Even though I wasn't supposed to go out to yard this morning, the officer let me. I smoked, played 'Simon Says' and 'Mother, May I?' I took some flowers, pressed them & will be sending them ASA I can. I played Scrabble & whooped ass, as usual. My two friends from County are here and I have another good friend Christine. You can look her & me up on the DOC [Department of Corrections] website. Please print mine out!

It's now **August 2**. I'm watching "Borat." I played WHORE in the yard instead of HORSE. Then I did 2 sets of 10 squats & lunges and 10 jumping jacks. I'm reading a Dan Brown book called *Deception Point*. My other book is *Gift From the Sea*. I want to get it for everyone for Xmas.

August 2 Nighttime

Song: The Widow (put on my Facebook), Artist: The Mars Volta
Mood: reflective, meditative, repentant

OMG there was just a big thunder boom that sounded like it was right outside the window & now they're running the generators. Lightning is exhilarating. Damn, most lights are back on. I was thinking, "Smoke Break," then "Prison Break!" J/K. Angels are bowling & God is crying tears of forgiveness, mercy, & joy that we ask for redemption.

Good night, Mama, Sleep Tight, Sweet Dreams!

August 3, 2009

Hey Ma! I saw the mental health evaluator. She asked lots of questions but didn't offer much help. I don't know if the Lamictal is working but being so stressed in here it's hard to tell. I'm sorry for worrying you so much about what I'm going through, I just wish I could write you every day & get a letter from you every day & maybe someone else for once in my life. I wish I was allowed to call my family, oh well. I guess I'll have plenty of time to talk to the people who have time to talk to a loser addict, dead beat mom in 23-27 months. Please write everyone I know & tell them my state address. I'm hurtin' here, Mama.

Love, Liz

August 3, 2009: Elizabeth's letter from Edna Mahan Correctional Facility to friend DJ in NJ State Male Prison

Song: Big Girls Don't Cry, Artist: Fergie
Mood: stressed, anxious, lonely, on Klonopin!

Hey DJ!

I miss you, I miss you, but I can't see you, so I'll kiss you through the mail. Nichole told me you got sentenced. I forgot 4 how long? 3 flat? Write me ASAP. I'm getting by. I just want you to know I'll always love you. 'They're comin' for us! They'll never catch us!' We had some good times, some bad times, and some real dirty, nasty times and I long for them all again! I got my PED [parole eligibility date] – 9/14/09! I got LORP [Loss of Rec Privileges] the first couple of days I got here – this bitch cop singles out the cute ones. How r the kids? Get back to me soon, I love you, you'll always be my partner cuz we're 2 of the craziest motherfuckers I know. Keep your chin up buttercup butt! XOXO

Love, Always & Forever, Lizabeth

[Sadly, DJ overdosed and died several years after Elizabeth died]

August 4, 2009: Things to do Before I Die (or Bucket List)

raise my son & teach him well
speak fluent French y Spanish
be an MMA fighter
get a college degree
get more tats
have a slammin' body
become a yoga guru
write my memoirs
make music & art
become a gnarly surfer
have dos mas hijos – L'Wren & Wiley
have a dream wedding
make my dad proud
fall in love
find my soul mate – please look 4 Matt
own a home
be a pregnant model
design clothes

What do you think Ma? Love, Little Lizzie

August 5, 2009: Letter from Edna Mahan Maximum Security

Songs: Here Comes the Sun & Mr. Blue Sky, Artists: The Beatles & ELO
Mood: excited, relieved, anxious, grateful, pensive

Dear Mommy, <u>mom</u> , <u>mama</u>, **Mom, mummy**, **MA!** [from *Family Guy*]

I got your mail w/ the $30 enclosed! Thank you so much! I know you went to a lot of trouble to get it for me. I look forward to hearing my name called and the caring thoughts you enclose w/ articles etc. I can't wait until we can have a visit. (NO GLASS or PHONES like county jail) so you can give your baby girl a big hug. I know I'll cry. I got a letter from Colleen w/ a sweet card & she sent me some $.

August 6

Song: Simple Man, Artist: Lynyrd Skynyrd
Mood: relieved, spiritual, blessed, loved

Hola Mamacita! So I'm finally out of f***in' reception. Praise the Lord!! I've been reading Psalms – Read Psalm 6 & 31. I met some really cool people. A Rastafarian who lives in Cali off the grid. I'm gonna get in touch w/ her when I get out 2 learn about organic farming & the Rastafari religion. Oh, my friend Christine told me about a zombie walk. It's in Philly around Easter (maybe you could come with?) & everyone dresses as zombies & walks down the street.

Song: Beautiful Day Artist: U2
Mood: chillin' out maxin' relaxin' all cool

Well I got to chill outside, smoke some cigs, talk 2 my
favorite mommy. I had 2 do my weekly chore: taking the
air vents from the top of the walls, taking them outside,
hosing them down, getting all the dust out and the CO was
messing around with me. He said "[last name], are you
smart?" I said, "Yes." He says, "The dumb ones usually say
that." I said, "I got 1400 on my SATs & scholarships to 2
colleges." He says, "What, Monmouth County?" I said,
"No – _____ & _____." He says, "What
did you major in?" I say, "I double-majored in apparel
design & merchandising." He says, "Well it's not a
fashionable chore, but it's fashionable to be clean."
Anyway, he jokes around & fucks w/ people all in good
fun.

Love, Lizzie

August 7, 2009: Letter from Edna Mahan Maximum Security

Song: Nobody Loves Me, Artist: Portishead
Mood: dejected, lonesome, losing my grip

Dear Mother,

I received your card sent July 30th, and what was inside
made me cry. I wrote heartfelt letters to family I love and
all I get back are a comment from Debbie about what a
great summer she's having, a 1-liner from the grandfather I
idolize, and zip, zilch, zero, nada, nil from Uncle Jim or
Grammy. I guess they really have lost all faith in me. Well I
can always just find a new family, one who can forgive or

122

maybe even look past my mistakes instead of taking my heart & soul on paper & giving me back rejection & inconsequential words.

I am constantly picked on, singled out, by female guards & all inmates. Two inmates have already screamed & cussed & threatened to beat my ass if I so much as look at them. What's the point. I may as well give up on ever getting my baby back if my family can't spare me more than 3 sentences or 44 cents for stamps. <u>I never meant to hurt anyone & I wish they would stop calling me a goddamn fucking HARDCORE DRUG ADDICT</u>. Fuck the world, fuck the police, fuck God, & fuck forgiveness, bc no one will forgive my sorry pathetic state property ass.

Love, Your Daughter

X DO NOT CALL HERE ABOUT THIS **X**
It will make it 10xs worse – I've just gotta get thicker skin.

PS Several inmates are making me give them stuff, food, toilet paper, (which we have to buy) to get a light or just cuz they wanna show how tough they are.

can't show them my tears
or own up to my fears
I don't know what I'm doing here
this forsaken part of the hemisphere
 I thought I could handle
but the flame to the candle
was too much to bear
want to rip out my hair
I fantasize
all the time
about taking a blade
like a jack of all trades
and slicing that vein

123

release all of my pain
forever and always
it'll be done, no take aways

August 10, 2009: Letter from Edna Mahan Maximum Security

Morning Mom – I just got a fucking blue sheet, BAD, so I'll probably be in Max for a while. Maybe 2 months. I tried to save my meds 4 after breakfast bc they hurt my stomach if I don't eat. They saw a pill in my mouth & it was dissolving so it stuck. Anyway this bitch makes me stay until the sgt. comes & they have a zero tolerance policy. **[The Official Institutional Discipline offense is Misuse of Authorized Medication – 60 additional days in Maximum Security]**.

August 14

Hey My Dear Mommie!

I was so glad to get to talk to you this evening! I miss you so much. Hopefully on the next round of visits, we'll be able to get our picture taken. I've lost weight but I'm still very jiggly & now I have stretch marks on my best **ass**et. Anyway, I'm working on writing a letter to Riley, you can email it to Axel if you like. Oh, and I forgot to tell you, I picked out a book for my "Project Storybook." I get 10-15 minutes to read a book aloud & sing a song & write a letter for Riley. I picked *Runaway Bunny*. So I talked to some people in similar situations, & they all agree w/ me that I should work on myself, immerse myself in reading & writing. That's all for now, I'm sleepy mama. Good night, sleep tight, don't let the bedbugs bite.

Love, your Little Lizzie

August 17, 2009: Letter from Edna Mahan Maximum Security

Song: Anticipation, Artist: Carly Simon
Mood: anxious to get my commissary, pissed off about racist bitches, anticipating this Saturday!

Dear Ma,

I'm busy playing Rummy 5000, getting my hair did (little braids in front, the rest is straightened). I finished *Of Human Bondage* and I'm almost finished *Lullaby* by Chuck Palahniuk (highly recommend it!) The librarian is awesome. She's been here goin' on 30 years and has read pretty much all the books in the Max library. You're only supposed to take 3-4 books out at a time but she lets me have 7!

I'm just working on myself, not getting caught up in drama & fights. This morning, just after breakfast there was almost a fight over who would use the WASHER first!?!! The white girl Shannon, should have gone, but the black lady, YaYa, said she didn't give a fuck, she'd throw the white bitch under the bunk, their faces touched, finally someone broke it up, otherwise there would have been a riot, b vs. w. I can't stand it. I wish I had a radio to drown it out. All this insanity! Sometimes people pick fights, right b/f they leave just because this is the only home they know or pick fights w/ people who are leaving soon bc they're angry it's not them. This is insanity, Mommy. Sometimes the officers over the P.A. system will make bird/monkey sounds all through their shift! OMG …what an insanely mangled web I've woven my life into.

I miss U, I love U, can't wait til Saturday ! I should get our picture forms tomorrow, so on Saturday look pretty – hair, makeup, clothes, etc. Pretty pretty please w/ Chubby Hubby [Ben & Jerry's] on top! I talked to my therapist yesterday. They are starting a DBT [Dialectical Behavioral Therapy] group bc I mentioned it to her! I may not be here to do it but am signing up for what I can. I'm counting the days til your visit. I want a big hug.

Love Liz

August 21, 2009: My Mommy's 47th B-day Letter from Edna Mahan Maximum Security

Song: Birthday, Artist: The Beatles

Hey Ma! Feliz Cumpleanos! My mommy is so beautiful inside & out. I'm such a lucky little lizzie! I had a <u>wonderful</u> bittersweet visit w/you yesterday. I just wanted to hug u the whole time!

I'm sorry I was so stressed about $ & everything. Anyway, I really appreciate your sacrificing so I don't get my ass whooped!! I'll spend this $ wisely mama, I promise! Maura, Tara & I are sharing everything, I'm buying 25 stamps & I hope to quit smoking by the time I get out.

Another beautiful day in EMCF. Did I tell you sometimes hot air balloons fly overhead, so low that they make us go inside? Oh, we have 2 little bunnies outside our window. Also a skunk & lots of deer. It was so cold a few days ago, I thought summer was over! I'm sorry that I don't have much to say, just that I miss you every day & I love you <u>soo</u> much. Oh, I got the picture of Riley! I can't BELIEVE how big my little baby is! He's so cute & fat & his eyes are big beautiful baby blues! He looks silly on that mini-bike.

Anyway, I hope you had a wonderful time for your b-day. You sounded happy w/ family & friends there. It was nice to talk to Aunt Meghan & Val.

126

Elizabeth, what are you going to do after you get out of Edna Mahan Correctional Facility? "I'm gonna stay clean, find the strength w/in myself to get my baby back, go get that paper ($) & I'm going to Disney World!"

Later, Lil' Lizzie

September 2, 2009: Letter from Edna Mahan Maximum Security

Song: Blow up the outside world, Artist: Soundgarden
Mood: anxious, weepy, missing everything – happier me, Riley, my mommy, the outside world

Dear Bestest Friend,

I miss you Mama. I'm so panic filled & anxiety stricken today that I can hardly handle anything. I'm sorry I haven't felt like writing since they've taken me off my meds, all I really do is read & chill in my bunk. I haven't even gone to the library. Everyone is like, "What's wrong with you?" I'm trying to do my best at getting up & writing, etc. but I really don't feel like doing anything.

They stopped my Celexa last week and I'm breaking down. I slept through breakfast & woke up with an upset tummy and feeling as though I could burst into tears at any moment. I saw the psychiatrist (finally) at 10am. He told me he stopped my Klonopin because he was told I was trying to cheek it a 2nd time. I told him I need it, the last thing I would do was try to sell it! He said they'll try Vistaril. I told him I've tried it, it doesn't work. He said he'd refill my Celexa, give me 100 mg Vistaril 2 xs a day & keep my Lamictal. I was like, "What if it doesn't work?" He said, "We'll see what happens." I'm basically bedridden. Now I know I'm agoraphobic. Yeah, I'll leave to go smoke but I'm just not the same, as everyone reminds

127

me. I can't wait to get out of here and get back on my meds & stop living like I don't value my life.

I just had my first parole hearing. He referred me to a panel as a result of my blue sheet [pill stuck on roof of her mouth]. It was my mistake – I'm suffering the consequences.

Love, Liz

September 3, 2009: Letter from Edna Mahan Maximum Security

Song: Me & Bobby McGee, Artist: Janis Joplin
Mood: nostalgic & connected

Hey Mama,

I started singing "Bobby McGee" in my head. That's one of the few songs I could listen to a million times & every time it churns up emotions, I feel it in my chest & my heart swells, what a beautiful feeling. It still astounds me that me, you, & your mom have that common thread – that song. I was thinking about us on the road. When we drove the Apache Trail, listening to old WDOX tapes. So much fun w/ you mom. I treasure those memories. I think of you and Riley constantly… of the family things we'll do together somewhere down the road. Please get me lyrics to "Bobby McGee" & to "Piece of My Heart". **[Elizabeth stopped writing for a visit from her mother, then continued after.]**
I can't begin to tell you how happy I was when they called my name for visits! I'm sorry I looked a hot mess. I'm sorry I interrupted w/all my drama about here & leaving etc.! I realized that for the first time in my adult life, I am completely single. I'm proud of myself. I've gotten letters from guys in jail but you'll be happy to know

128

that I haven't replied. I'm sincerely trying to make the most of this "alone time" and embrace what independence I have, (yes in prison!) remember, "stone walls do not a prison make." From a poem ["To Althea, From Prison" by Richard Lovelace] I have in the humongous mass of papers I've accumulated thus far. I think maybe in my 40's or 50's, I'll start my own rehab…capitalize on all the $ & knowledge that has been doled out on my behalf. Sound like a plan? Well it's 12 AM now… lights out…

Love, your Little Girl

September 13, 2009: Letter from Edna Mahan Maximum Security

Song: Angel of Harlem, Artist: U2
Mood: bored, boring, industrious

!Hola Mamacita!

How are you this evening? Thank you for the pictures. This girl Tara from my county, well her parents both died of AIDS & she was talking about Janis Joplin & how her mom loved her, so I sang "Piece of My Heart" for her & she said she got chills!

Guess what I saw last night? Fireworks! Don't know what they were for, but they were beautiful. Someone got scared & heard someone knocking on the window, got us all freaked out & then we looked out the window & to our delight, fireworks! It was the vibrations from the explosives making the tapping noise. It went on for an hour! It was a nice treat & it was so close it felt like it was just for us criminals. Haha! Well I miss you & can't wait to see you & please please please get $ from Jimmy G & Bobby. I need $100 a month to survive in here – my feet are full of blisters from the awful boots. Please inform Jimmy G of this. I want to send this out ASAP.

xoxo ♥ Lil'Lizzie

September 21, 2009: Letter from Edna Mahan Maximum Security

Song: New York (incredible song, must download – LISTEN TO LRYICS!), Artist:Jay-Z
Mood: hyper, grateful, hopeful

!Hola Mamacita!

How are you? I'm trying to practice my mindfulness & live in the present moment – a la Marsha Linehan. I am devouring books – love Harlan Coben – and I'm reading *Eat, Pray, Love* again, so insightful & comforting; 38 days...I think it's healthy to be nervous because I'll be losing a lot if I return to my "active addict" self. I am learning about myself in here...I do isolate but that is how I cope... I don't want to "shoot the shit" & glamorize that drug & criminal lifestyle anymore. In reality, I had more bad days when I was using than fun. I try to recollect the times I was crying & agonizing. I'm sorry you had to see me that way, but I need to remember & I hope it gave you a view of the struggle to stay clean. I miss my best friend, I can't wait to see you ASAP! "I want my mommy!!" I'm always worrying about something going wrong. I may be going to grounds [out of maximum security] next week. I hope so – it's getting to be too much here in max. I just did yoga & I feel <u>soo</u> much better. You really do get a natural high from it. Well I've got to get this in the mail ASAP! My thoughts are with you, Ma. I can't wait to talk to you & to see you without khakis [uniform]!

Love You Lots, xxoo, Little Lizzie

October 20, 2009: Letter from Edna Mahan

Song: Lockdown, Artist: Kanye
Mood: relieved, miss my mommy!!

Mommy Dearest!

I was so happy that I <u>FINALLY</u> got to talk to you! I
wish we had more time. I know you're worried about me &
what I'm going to do when I get out of this hellhole. <u>But</u> – I
do not want you to put unnecessary stress on yourself. I
will be out in 9 days & no matter where I go, I recognize
that it's going to be a struggle & I must be vigilant because
addiction as we know is cunning, baffling, & powerful. I
spoke to the nice parole lady & she told me that they will
put me in placement & I must report to the parole office as
soon as I get out. It's my responsibility NOT YOURS to
ensure that I find a suitable place to live so that I don't end
up back here.

I can't believe I'm finally getting out – I do not take that
for granted – if I screw up, I'll be here til 2012. I'm asking
you not to put so much pressure on me because I put so
much on myself already & so does the State of New Jersey.
If I'm going to do this, I need to be my own master – not a
slave to my former lifestyle. I dream about cooking a
yummy dinner – my homemade mac & cheese, tollhouse
pie.

I've been doing yoga at least once a day to get into the
habit of something healthy, stress releasing, & centering.
I've been practicing meditation & mindfulness as well. I
make sure to use positive self-talk. I thank God probably 3x
a day for all my blessings because despite being locked up,
I'm grateful for so much. Especially you, ma. I'm sending
along letters I wrote last month, I forget what they said-I

hope they're still current. I miss you big fat bunches. I wonder if there is some way that we could get a 2BR so we could live together but not bother each other. Just an idea. Please stop stressing. I will deal w/ parole. I'm forever grateful but I need to grow up & take the driver's seat in my life. Please make sure my Daddy picks me up October 29th as close to 6:30AM as possible. I have so much more to talk about w/ you but I'll save that for in person.

Love & Hugs & Kisses to all, Elizabeth xxoo

Parole, Parole Violated, and Garrett Halfway House

Undated Poem by Elizabeth

I'm a sub-human
who is roomin'
in a dope motel
on the outskirts of hell

October 29, 2009

Elizabeth's original parole situation/address – a friend in North Jersey was going to give her a place to live and a job at his restaurant – fell through. So, Parole sent her to a cheap drug motel for a week.

Elizabeth used heroin and crack on the night she got out on parole and her parole officer found her on November 4, 2009. She admitted she'd been using. The parole officer brought her in on violation of parole and took her to Garrett House, a NJ Department of Corrections halfway back house in Camden, NJ for prisoners and parolees.

November 10, 2009: Elizabeth's Private Journal at Garrett House, Camden, NJ

When I'm sober, I feel like the world is full of endless opportunities. Yet when I'm out on the "streets," it all seems so far out of reach. I wonder if I'll ever stop wanting to get high.

133

I just talked to Axel & Riley. I feel like running & never stopping. I want to fill up this hole in my soul with all the food/ sex /drugs/clothes that I can – because I think I'll always be lost. I feel like I let Axel ruin me for whatever life can offer. How can I ever be a mother to Riley again? How can I ever be in a healthy relationship w/out bringing my boatloads of baggage w/ me?

November 12, 2009: Initial Communication from Austin, future Parole Address friend

Hey Elizabeth,

I talked to your mom on your myspace and she told me to write to you. Apparently, she worked at the pre-school I went to, and you were there with me. It's a small world. Well, I'm Austin, and I hope you get the chance to write back. I think we can relate alotttt! I just spent 7 months in military confinement for use, distro, [distribution] and conspiracy to distro a controlled substance. How long did you get and how much longer do you have? If you need anything, don't be afraid to write and ask! I know how it is. I got out in May and am on probation until next October. I can't wait to have it over for good. If I can come visit, let me know. Is there anything you need/want right now? Sorry for the short letter but I wanted to say "Hi." I hope you write back soon!

Talk to you soon, Austin

November 14, 2009: Elizabeth's Private Journal at Garrett House, Camden, NJ

I think back to all the men I was with last week…about how I take a piece of their soul with me when they release. I can see through them…I know who is good and who is evil. Sometimes I find myself comforted by the most unlikely guy…I reward him with a little piece of me; I let him hold me, let him hold on to the illusion that I care, that I am attracted to him, that he satisfies me. Maybe a part of me is satisfied because it reminds me of another time, when I slept with men who I let get to know me, as much as I could allow, & they loved me regardless. Then when I was done with them I took their pride & trust & ego & crumpled it like a scrap of paper in my fist. They realized it was all a game. When I knew they were addicted, strung out on my drug, I left them alone, sick, withdrawing, longing for the feel of that first hit.

November 16, 2009: Elizabeth's Private Journal at Garrett House

I'm listening to Pink's "Who Knew?" a song that really speaks to me about my marriage to Axel. I still hold onto a lot of love for him. As I know the opposite of love is not hate, it is indifference. I long for the good times we had, the laughs, the time spent with family, the intimate moments. It's like my memory erases the bad things that went along with it, kind of like drugs do.

He was just like a drug to me.

November 24, 2009: Sheila visits Elizabeth at Garrett House

Elizabeth was so happy to see me when I got there that she started crying. I had brought a lot of her stuff and a piece of pumpkin pie I'd made for her. We went down to the lounge to visit.

Elizabeth said to me, "Can you tell?"

I said, "What?"

She said, "I used today."

I said, "What did you use?"

Elizabeth, "Guess."

I said "Heroin."

Elizabeth, "Yes."

I asked Elizabeth if she wasn't worried about getting caught and she said no, she had pills for that, but she didn't think they would test her anyway.

Elizabeth told me she did not want to stop using and would use substances they didn't test for. They only tested for cocaine, opiates, and weed – she said she could use Xanax, Klonopin, and alcohol. Elizabeth constantly carried on her person tools to fool the test. Evidently, she had already passed one drug test (while using heroin) by flushing with green tea – just on a hunch.

Elizabeth told me she was constantly seriously considering running from the Garrett House and becoming a fugitive. She had not had her mood stabilizer or her antidepressant for three days because her prescription ran out. This house was contracted with the state as part of the prison system and obviously the low bid won. There were no groups, no meetings, no treatment whatsoever – except one Sunday meeting out of the house.

Out on the street, Elizabeth had gotten a needle that looked like a pen. She had also bought a few prescription pills. Elizabeth told me again she didn't want to stop using. She thought she could function as a heroin addict, as long as she avoided crack. I told her I understood that she alone could decide when she wanted to attempt to stop using, but I reminded her that she needed to get through 18 months of parole.

One nice moment was when Elizabeth told me that she wished she had been more open and honest with me when she was a teenager.

Elizabeth was crying when I left, and she asked me why *I* wasn't crying. I didn't know what to say. I felt numb with the shock of seeing her high on heroin in a prison halfway house – I was afraid she would get another drug charge. She was like, "I miss you more than you miss me." She wanted me to stay, she wanted to come with me, she wanted me to take her home, she just wanted to live with her mommy like it used to be…it was heart wrenching.

November 27, 2009: Elizabeth's Private Journal at Garrett House

I had a very fulfilling visit w/my mommy tonight – after my disastrous period of being off my psych meds, I finally am starting to feel like myself again. I do admit that part of me liked the highs & creativity of the mania, but the despair I experienced in the lows was incomparable.

I'm glad I didn't leave. I want to be positive. **I will write my story** & realize my dreams. I will organize my life, my mind, my connectedness w/ others. My ma & I laughed a lot – at [stepbrother's] card to me, at lots of stuff. I got over the disappointment of ending the visit.

November 28, 2009: Sheila visits Garrett House

I arrived at Garrett House. Elizabeth and I went downstairs to visit. Elizabeth immediately told me she desperately needed my help. She had possession of a Suboxone tablet and had put it down her pants to hide it and she flushed it down the toilet by mistake. Elizabeth said she owed a girl ½ of the pill, and if she did not give it to this girl, the girl would beat her up.

Elizabeth begged me to score her a Suboxone on the streets of Camden. I freaked out. I couldn't imagine how many laws I would be breaking, (bringing a controlled substance into a Department of Corrections halfway house), plus Camden was the murder capital of the U.S.

Elizabeth was sobbing and I was afraid of her getting beat up. So eventually, feeling stupid, angry, scared… I

137

agreed to do it. She drew me a diagram of where to go and coached me on how to behave in order to score. She gave me a $10 bill and I left. I felt like I was losing my mind. I felt numb. I walked where she told me to walk. Someone came up to me and asked what I wanted. I said I wanted a Suboxone tablet. The guy said he didn't have one with him, but he could go get one. So I gave him the $10. Of course he never came back.

I don't even remember the rest of the visit or the drive home. I felt this was the first time Elizabeth had taken advantage of me and put me in danger. I was angry and hurt.

November 28, 2009: Elizabeth's Private Journal at Garrett House

I must be the biggest piece of shit that ever lived.
I jeopardized my best friend for drugs.

November 29, 2009: Elizabeth's Private Journal at Garrett House

I made my mom do something that was against her morals.
I feel bad but I think I've reached a new low.
I miss my Mommy so much. She visited again today – I was afraid she wouldn't. I feel like we should always be near each other. Maybe that's my abandonment issues.
Austin surprised me with a visit. It was kind of awkward with them both there. My mom agreed to leave after a while to give us some time alone. Austin says I remind him of Megan Fox. As we were walking up the stairs, he pulled me close. We really had good 'kiss' chemistry.

December 7, 2009: Garrett House

Elizabeth was caught having sex on the job. She lost visiting privileges. She has to stay in her room and can only come down to use the phone for ten minutes a day. But Elizabeth told me she had a good meeting with her case manager and the director of the halfway house. They realize she has serious problems and are going to try to get her a sex addiction counselor. She's hopeful.

December 9, 2009: Moved from Garrett House to Bo Robinson

Elizabeth's case manager from Garrett House called me. Her parole officer had come and taken her to Bo Robinson, a NJ DOC Assessment & Treatment Center in Trenton. This facility was a step back in terms of freedom and reentry into the community. It was locked. Her case manager said Elizabeth had received four sanctions in 14 days:
1. 15 minutes late calling in after a job interview
2. A failed drug test
3. Sex with fellow employee on the job
4. An unauthorized stop at the post office to cash a money order

Bo Robinson Prison Assessment and Treatment Center

Undated Poem by Elizabeth

who does this shit?
every day, find a way
to further complicate it
my name is Elizabeth
I am an addict
what's my drug of choice?
any & every habit

December 12, 2009: Elizabeth's Private Journal at Bo Robinson

So right now I'm sitting in the lovely, accommodating Bo Robinson kicking Suboxone & Xanax. I don't think I've ever slept this much. When I'm awake, it feels like my mind is short circuiting. I feel the synapses in my brain misfiring and fizzling out. I keep having these really vivid dreams. I'm not on Celexa right now. The dreams leave such an impression on me that it makes me think that the creativity I thought was gone is just being clouded by all my medication.

December 14, 2009: Elizabeth's Private Journal at Bo Robinson

Wow… I love my life… I love my life… I LOVE MY LIFE… now can I click my heels 3 times & make it so? This is the <u>CONSEQUENCES</u> of my using and trying to continue my criminal lifestyle while my soul is still owned by NJ State Parole Board. So I managed to fuck up again.

December 16, 2009: Elizabeth's Private Journal at Bo Robinson

Three years ago tonight I was in Las Vegas, drinking a bottle of Moet to work up the courage to marry Axel. I guess I'm still mourning the death of the happily ever after I thought I would be living. Will I ever get over it?

I'm listening to Elliot Smith now – "New Moon." What a fucking genius. When I'm listening to quality music that speaks to my soul, I feel like anything is possible.

I yearn for the intimacy of lying in bed talking. I'm struggling with the fact that I have no contact with the outside world – no mail, no phone calls – none of those reassurances that I thrive on. No proof that I matter to anyone. I find myself living in my fantasy world again. It's what drives me to keep going, and I guess I've done it all my life. Living in my mind because I don't tend to do it so successfully in real life.

December 17, 2009: Elizabeth's Private Journal at Bo Robinson

Sometimes I look at myself and think I'm beautiful, is that why Austin wants me? I'm sick of that, like bc I'm nice to look at, a man thinks I'm the answer to his problems or prayers or whatever. I want someone to get to know the real me. (who the fuck is that anyway? the little girl; the

142

mother; the temptress; the wife; the geek; the one who breaks all the rules; the confident chick cracking jokes with the guys; the bipolar, bulimic, wrist-cutting mental patient; the street smart whore sitting in prison; the positive, trusting, compassionate woman who knows she's meant for better things; maybe just the sullen girl who feels at home all alone with her music…and then come the drugs.) How do I find out who I am?

December 18, 2009: Elizabeth's Private Journal at Bo Robinson

It seems that, as usual, I've been living in a land of make believe. I don't rate in people's lives as much as I thought…still no mail. I'm fucking retarded to think that Austin even gives a shit whether I live or die. And my dumb ass put his house down as my address for parole. All I wanna do is cry & scream & be held, but all I can do is sit on my green fucking bunk & try to stifle my tears. It just goes to show that I have absolutely nothing to go home to.

Fuck falling in love, there I am, trusting in someone I hardly know AGAIN. Alright, no more fucking tears, pussy. Suck it up, buttercup. Ok, I'm beautiful, smart, I know how to survive ALL BY MYSELF. Who wants to risk getting their heart broken? I need to plan my next move.

December 22, 2009: Elizabeth's Private Journal at Bo Robinson

mood: BAH HUMBUG!

Christmastime at Bo. I hate this uncertainty. I am eligible to leave on February 4th. Please God, they have broken me already, I understand that these are my consequences of my using. I know I can follow the rules…until I am off parole, at least. I don't know where

I'm gonna go after I get out of here. My mom wants me to go back to Garrett House...what, with my tail between my legs, forced to kiss ass in a place where they've all made up their minds about who I am?

I was obviously suffering from a bout of naiveté when I thought Austin was serious about me. Stuck without a parole address, yet again. Why do I always think men are telling the truth. Will I ever learn? It's just me against the world.

December 23, 2009: Assigned Journal for her Counselor at Bo Robinson

I like the word of the day, "control," because using drugs is all about control. If I don't like the mood I'm in, I can bring it up or down whenever I want. This is so unhealthy because you never have to really sit with how you're feeling, which means you are just deflecting all of your problems, yet when you come down, those problems are still there...yet most likely are worse. I have no control over being at Bo, but I can continue to keep the focus on myself, **write the story of my life,** & understand that the ending is all up to me.

December 24, 2009: Elizabeth's Private Journal at Bo Robinson

♫ Kill me please, I'm on my knees. I hate my life. I'm all excited to finally get some fucking mail, like a dumbass, and my mom drops the bomb that she won't be coming. Merry Christmas. You might as well kill yourself because no one gives a shit. Wow. Am I that torturous to be around? So I got my little cry on for a few minutes. Now I'm back to "I'm gonna harden my heart, I'm gonna swallow my tears." She slips in an email from Austin. He says he'll try to come after Xmas. Praise God and six lb. 7 ounce baby

144

Jesus in his diapers. I guess I deserve it for what I did to her [begged mom to score suboxone] the last time I saw her. Oh well, enough self-loathing for one night, suck it up Buttercup.

Christmas Eve, 2009: Letter from Bo Robinson

Song: Sour Times, Artist: Portishead
Mood: distraught, depressed, lonely

Mother,

So I'm already stressing because I'm here and all I've been looking forward to since Thanksgiving has been seeing you on Christmas. So I'm happy because they finally call my name for mail & I open the letter only to be disappointed beyond belief. I had actually set some ground rules for myself concerning how I would act during the visit. I wasn't going to ask for anything – money, calls, clothes, etc. I know you know how much it would mean for me to see my family on Christmas. And no, I don't know that you love me – because if you did, all you'd want to do was see me. That's just how I feel. All I want to do right now is say some really hurtful things to you so you will feel how I do. I won't.

I'm just going to get out of here as soon as I can, live my life, clean & sober, go back to school, and get through parole. It's just me, myself, and I, and I suppose I deserve it, I just thought we had a better relationship than that. Thank you for the presents. You should be laughing and eating dessert right now. Enjoy yourself. It's time I stood on my own and learned not to rely on anyone else. Merry Christmas.

Love, Your Daughter

A girl's gotta have big shoulders
to carry all these boulders
anything you can imagine
there's always something worse
here comes the river
as I shake & shiver
my fate depends on this card
will life always be so hard?
Reality is red
Forgiveness is dead

Christmas Day, 2009: Assigned Journal for her Counselor at Bo Robinson

Ugh, this is the worst Christmas I've ever had. Sitting around watching "A Christmas Story" – usually a tradition that my mom and I carry out, watching movies & opening gifts. I try not to think about Riley because that breaks my heart. As long as I do what I'm supposed to, this is the last Christmas I'll be all alone. This is usually my favorite time of year but it's definitely not "Merry" at Bo. If I feel the need to use, I need to remind myself to read my journal entries as a discouraging factor for getting high.

Today my mom was supposed to visit with my aunt and uncle. I got a letter saying that she's not coming. That she needs to give me distance after the last visit. I understand where she's coming from, but I can't help but feel like she's doing this <u>to hurt me</u>. I've always got to remind myself that she's mentally ill and doesn't always think things through. And it is true that she enmeshes her life with mine so much to the point that it is unhealthy. She does need to have her own identity. Still it hurts and I miss my family a lot today.

January 2, 2010: Assigned Journal for her Counselor at Bo Robinson

Today was awful. I heard my name being called for mail. I got a letter from my mom. She said that no one has picked up my stuff from Garrett House yet, so I'm pretty much guaranteed to have my iPod stolen. I can't believe how she's acting. I know I've been an a**hole, but she's always been there for me regardless. I suppose I deserve it. At least maybe I'll get the picture that I can't just keep on hurting people & expecting them to still be there, cheering me on.

January 5, 2010: Elizabeth's Worksheet today: Bo Robinson

> **Do you think your self-image has been affected by trauma?**
> Yes
>
> **Explain:**
> I have a lot of guilt over a traumatic event that I experienced. Growing up, I thought there was something wrong with me because of what happened. I felt flawed, shameful, and abnormal. It's hard to get past those self-inflicted labels that I attached to myself at such a young age. It takes a lot more effort to ingrain positive thoughts – now that I know it wasn't my fault. If I find myself using negative self-talk, I try to "flip the script" & negate negative thoughts with positive ones.
>
> **Do you find it easy to trust others?**
> No
>
> **Explain:**

147

I tend to isolate myself from others – withdraw into music and books, instead of socializing. Part of it has to do with my anxiety disorder, but it's also a fear that I can't trust others enough to get close to them without them hurting me. I'm reluctant to let my guard down because I feel if someone knows who I am, really, they won't like me. For some, it seems I tell too much, & I always regret it.

Did anyone ever abuse you physically or sexually as a child?
Yes

If so, describe how you felt:
I felt very ashamed afterward but it was a pleasurable physical feeling. I think mentally, it made me confuse sex with love.

January 6, 2010: Assigned Journal for her Counselor at Bo Robinson

I think that since I got divorced and started using again, my mom has felt guilty. She held herself partly responsible for my addiction. She allowed me to live recklessly at her apartment in Moab, and enabled me. Now that I've screwed up and taken advantage of her (which I'd never done before), she seems to be trying to put up some boundaries.

January 9, 2010: Assigned Journal for her Counselor at Bo Robinson

I still find myself longing for the past. Especially the good times I had when I was married. It's funny, even though I was miserable a lot, most of all when Axel was drinking, I find it hard to let go of that promise of happily ever after. At the time I really thought that was my destiny.

I believed everything Axel said. I believed we would be a happy family and continue to build our lives together. I'm struggling to recognize my identity now that I'm all alone.

January 10, 2010: Assigned Journal for her Counselor at Bo Robinson

How do I know if I am being true to myself? I don't really even know myself. The things that I've been capable of do not define who I think I am. I want to be strong, independent, confident, driven, admirable, and determined. It's hard to imagine how long it's going to take me to get back on my feet. I've really made an enormous mess of my life.

January 12, 2010: Assigned Journal for her Counselor at Bo Robinson

I had an unexpected delight tonight. I got a package from my mom. I feel so much better after reading her letter. I understand where she's coming from. I agree she needs to have a life. I'm glad we're working on a healthy mother/daughter relationship as opposed to friends/enabler.

January 12, 2010 Letter from Bo Robinson

!Hola Mamacita!

Let me start off by expressing my immeasurable gratitude for the two lovely packages. They made me <u>so</u> happy. The first one was great because when I left Garrett House I didn't get to bring toiletries w/me. (By the way, someone stole the deodorant you sent me). I love the pjs, so cute! They wouldn't let me have the playing cards or nail polish. The X-mas card was very touching. I would have liked to have gotten a visit, but I suppose that's my fault. I thought you were just gonna continue to ignore me, so imagine my surprise when I got the 2nd box yesterday! I was ecstatic! I said, "My Mommy still loves me!" I LOVE the Hello Kitty gel pens that you sent!

Well this place is definitely worse than anywhere I've been before. PERIOD. It's supposed to be a treatment center but I've only seen my counselor once in the 5 weeks that I've been here – just to fill out paperwork. The food is worse than the County Jail & the state prison. I'm always hungry.

We are required to keep a daily journal. My counselor asked to see mine today and looked over it and said it was one of the best she's seen in years. She said I should write a book & that I'm very insightful. I could go on for pages about how badly this place sucks ass but I want to send this out so you know how happy you made me! Thank you, THANK YOU! I miss you, please let me know what is going on with you, the family, the world. The last time I spoke to Austin was before New Year's. He told me he would come but never showed – and he is my parole address!! Now I really am all alone. Could you please send me some stamps so I can try to get in touch with someone, ANYONE? Thanks Mama! I miss you bunches, I'm so sorry I let everyone down again. I can only try to do what I need to do when I get out.

I've stopped ALL psych meds. Please write back NOW!

Love Your Loving Little Lizzie

January 13, 2010: Assigned Journal for her Counselor at Bo Robinson

Being here at Bo is really a lesson in humility and gratitude. You have to adapt to being without what you are used to, while being thankful for what God does provide – your basic needs.

150

Gratitude List
1.   My son is being well taken care of
2.   I have a roof over my head
3.   I have a bed to sleep in with pillows & blankets
4.   I have a book to read (sometimes)

January 15, 2010: Assigned Journal for her Counselor at Bo Robinson

I really enjoyed the meeting tonight. I could identify with every single one of the issues that the speaker mentioned: molestation and the guilt resulting from other early sexual encounters, cutting, eating disorder, jealousy, cheating, using sex for power, staying high to feel numb, etc.

January 17, 2010: Assigned Journal for her Counselor at Bo Robinson

So last night there was a fight in my room. It's really disappointing to see people take a step backward when they're so close to leaving & have got so much to lose. The tension and negative energy in the air was palpable. People feed off of it, it's contagious. I was very disturbed by the events that transpired and I'm finding it hard not to let it affect me today. I pray that God keeps me from dwelling on all this unpleasantness, and that he watches over those involved, as I'm sure they're beating themselves up over it.

January 19, 2010: Assigned Journal for her Counselor at Bo Robinson

I believe in the power of my dreams. Sometimes I find that I'm not at Bo at all…I'm surfing in Costa Rica, or giving hugs and kisses to Riley. If I don't follow a program

151

of recovery and do what parole wants, I will be giving up all those dreams. I want to be able to open my own Plato's Closet franchise, & definitely my own website. I must focus on my sobriety and bettering myself to make these dreams my reality.

Positive Affirmations
I am beautiful inside & out.
I am a Child of God.
I am worthy of love.
I am a good person despite my past mistakes.
I deserve to be happy.
I deserve to be loved unconditionally.
I can be whatever I want to be.
I have people who love me and care about me.
I will **write my own story.**
I forgive myself.

January 20, 2010: Assigned Journal for her Counselor at Bo Robinson

I am getting so frustrated in this miserable place. It is a constant struggle to keep others' negativity from affecting me. I have to keep telling myself that these are the consequences of my using and/or continuing to live a criminal lifestyle.

January 22, 2010: Assigned Journal for her Counselor at Bo Robinson

I had a good day! It's amazing what contact w/ the outside world can do. I got an unexpected letter from TJ this morning & it set a good tone. He's always very positive about recovery & inspires me. It's comforting to know that I have him as a support when I get out.

January 23, 2010: Assigned Journal for her Counselor at Bo Robinson

I finally got all the correspondence I had been waiting for. My mom wrote, my Pop-pop, and Austin. My mom's letter made me laugh, Pop-pop's brought tears to my eyes, and Austin's made me giddy. At least now I know my address is approved for parole. Once again, God takes care of my basic needs and then some. Austin has plans to go to some concerts. Thank God because I am going to need to stay busy when I first get out.

January 27, 2010: Assigned Journal for her Counselor at Bo Robinson

Being in this program has been one of the most uncomfortable & irritating consequences I've endured since being under the State of New Jersey's thumb. I only have myself to blame for my miserable surroundings. I think it needs to be so bad so that it's a deterrent from picking up drugs. I try to make the most of the time in here so that I can work on changing the things that brought me to places like this. I recognize that I have antisocial tendencies. It's hard to reconcile the fact that I live a criminal lifestyle.

January 28, 2010 Letter from Bo Robinson

Hello Best Mommy Ever!

That belated birthday card was hysterical. Unfortunately, no one here had the brain capacity to get it. LOL! I love getting mail from you, and I understand that you need to assert your boundaries, but please understand that I acknowledge them, and agree to respect them. There will be no need to discuss it any further. Now with that unpleasantness out of the way, let me tell you how happy it's made me to know that you will be picking me up! Austin was going to have to take off work & I am very grateful to be able to spend time w/ my BFF when I get out of <u>HELL</u>! Thank you in advance for bringing me cigarettes! I'm so excited to have a mini road trip w/ you & sing songs like we do. Did you get the box back w/ the cd player? Oh well, if not, that is one of the consequences of my using. I can tell you all the things I'm going to do in order to keep from using & going back to prison or relapsing but I need to start walking the walk, not just talking the talk. Oh, I forgot to tell you, Deanna is here w/ me, she says "Hi!" Also TJ got my address & we've been writing, he's always an inspiration. He has over 2 years clean & has a car so he said he can pick me up for meetings. Make sure you're here by 8:45AM on Thursday so I can be out by 9. Thank you so much! I miss you!

Love, Little Lizzie

February 3, 2010: Elizabeth's Private Journal Bo Robinson

So I just found out I'm not leaving tomorrow. I guess in the back of my mind I knew I couldn't count on this place. It's extremely frustrating to be at the mercy of incompetent individuals, namely Ms. M. I've only seen her once since I've been here, yet she holds the key to my freedom. That's one more reason not to let these m.f.'ers have me under their thumb again.

Parole Two

Undated Poem by Elizabeth

never wanted much
just all that I can't have
fantasies and such
lust for what I can't grab
unslakable thirst
insatiable hunger
to covet is worst
the days I was younger
manic desires
no doubt I will conquer
can't douse these flames
cuz I am the fever

Parole: February 10, 2010 to March 4, 2010

I picked Elizabeth up from Bo Robinson early on the
morning of February 10th 2010. We drove to Austin's
house, which was her parole address. Each morning she
had to report to the DRC (Day Reporting Center), as a
parole requirement.

Elizabeth's Facebook Status: February 10, 2010: "I'm
so sick and tired of trying to change your mind when it's so
easy to disconnect mine" ["High Times" by Elliott Smith]

February 11, 2010: Sheila's Lunch with Elizabeth

Elizabeth was severely stressed when I picked her up at Austin's to go have lunch. She was actually feeling guilty that she was not happier to be out of prison. She was like, "how long will I feel this totally stressed out, what can I do?" I gave her half a Klonopin [script], and I could see the difference in half an hour – it was like night and day.

I told her how proud I was that she didn't use heroin or crack last night or today in the city. She had already told me she had gotten drunk. I knew she would drink to attempt to alleviate her anxiety. I said I was proud of her because she made it to her parole appointment at 8:30am. They told her she could go home, and she did – even though she was tempted to stay in the city to make money, score drugs etc.

We had pizza, then I said I would spend $20 on snow boots that she needed. We didn't find boots, but I bought her hair dye, body lotion, and makeup – and gave her $ for food until Austin gets paid. I only spent two hours with Elizabeth today, but we were honest with each other.

We talked about the truth; she said, "why would I want to stop getting high?" I asked her if she ever truly wanted to get sober, and Elizabeth told me what I already knew – only BEFORE she met Axel, had Riley, and lost Riley. She feels she has lost Riley forever. Also, she was like, "with me and Axel as parents, he'll grow up to be an addict for sure." I told her genetic predisposition is only a part of it. Riley is not "doomed." But since losing Riley, she sees no real reason not to get high. Elizabeth said she feels awful all the time, why not get high? It is just logical to her. Why would she NOT get high?

After lunch I dropped her back at Austin's. I understand Elizabeth much better now. I saw how much half a Klonopin helped her. When I picked her up, I had said, "I can smell the alcohol coming out of your pores," and she said, "yeah, well I had a little 'hair of the dog' this morning, I had a hangover..." That is not a person who wants to be sober, and Elizabeth admits it.

This is Elizabeth's truth: She WISHES that she didn't want to use – however, that is ALL she thinks about – getting high.

> In my hot little hand I hold
> the key to never growing old
> as it radiates my senses yield
> I awaken in a flowering field
> novocaine for my brain
> lullaby within
> it pulls me under
> no more pain

I feel a bit less sad now that I understand Elizabeth does not WANT a "regular" life. She wants money, sex, drugs, excitement, expensive stuff. **<u>At this point in time</u>**, Elizabeth doesn't believe she wants a life without drugs.

As he had promised, Austin took Elizabeth to several concerts upon her release.

Elizabeth's Facebook Status February 13, 2010: last night: Drive A, Atreyu, and The Used....... the best homecoming ever

Elizabeth (NJ) and Matt (FL) Reconnect

Undated Poem by Elizabeth

> I'd like to hear whatever you have to say
> about your past, your future, your today
> and with every mustard seed I pray
> that your love for me will never sway
> I'll redeem my mistakes
> for both of our sakes
> I'll be your deviant fantasy
> and make it our forever reality

8:42pm, February 17, 2010 – Text from Matt to Elizabeth: Sorry liz! Every time u call me…im somewhere ridiculously loud

11:44pm, February 17, 2010 – Text from Elizabeth to Matt: Hey how was ur meeting babe? luv u

8:29pm, February 18, 2010– Text from Matt to Elizabeth: Love u, love u, love u, ur the sexiest bitch ever!! I can't wait 4 u 2 b in my arms again!!

8:54 pm, February 18, 2010– Text from Elizabeth to Matt: Be my belated valentine? am gonna talk 2 parole about transferring down to Florida asap xoxo

11:33pm, February 18, 2010 – Text from Elizabeth to Matt: Wish i could wake up in ur arms. Have sweet and sick dreams of me

11:41pm, February 18, 2010 – Text from Matt to Elizabeth: U r the cats pajamas!!Hurry up and come back 2 me my lost love!!!!

1:37pm, February 19, 2010 – Text from Elizabeth to Matt: Hey, sitting in group & saw my parole officer… pissed 4 him, he was takin' bets that i'd be dirty – haha, i'm clean biotch. i told him i wanna move down to florida, he said i need 2 move in with family or spouse and will take 3 to 6 months

1:43pm, February 19, 2010 – Text from Matt to Elizabeth: So just marry me!!

1:45pm, February 19, 2010 – Text from Elizabeth to Matt: I deserve a better proposal than that baby

1:49pm, February 19, 2010 – Text from Matt to Elizabeth: I wouldn't propose 2 u in a txt msg baby!! I just want u down here w me!! U r sooo beautiful…ur firecrackers on the 4th!

1:56pm, February 19, 2010 – Text from Elizabeth to Matt: Your love is better than disney world. I want to get tha fuck outta dirty jersey w/u, so help me figure it out

2:16pm, February 19, 2010 – Text from Matt to Elizabeth: I would die 4 u…kill and steal 4 u…i would wash away ur pain with all my tears!!! ["#1 Crush" by Garbage]

8:28pm, February 19, 2010 – Text from Matt to Elizabeth: If i had a shotgun…u know what i'd do? I'd point that shit straight at the sky, and shoot heaven on down 4 u!! ["Don't Push" by Sublime]

8:47pm, February 19, 2010 – Text from Elizabeth to Matt: We must have espn bc i was yearning to hear that from u again my love 4ever. -espn = extra sensuality pertaining 2matt & liz naturally

February 20, 2010: Prodigal Sons & Daughters Parole Worksheet

Write down the names of four very successful people:
1. My Pop-pop
2. Bob Marley
3. Ben Harper
4. Jenna Jameson

Write down six characteristics you believe have contributed to their success:
1. Creativity
2. Dependability
3. Boldness
4. Decisiveness
5. Contentment
6. Attentiveness

What is your highest goal in life? What do you want? What would make you happy?
To be happy in recovery; I want to be happy & secure in my relationships; have enough $ to be able to follow my dreams & be generous; having a healthy, happy family would make me happy.

Who would you want to share in that happiness with you?

My significant other, my children, parents, brother, family and friends

What must you do to acquire that happiness?
Work the steps, stay out of jail, go back to school, find my passion, find a lucrative career

Are you prepared to do what is necessary to achieve your goal?
Yes, I am ready to start a new chapter in my life.

Is there anything you want more, or is more important to you?
I want my son Riley back (<u>full</u> custody)

What adjustments must you make right away to get started?
Stay clean, attend college, do what parole wants, stay focused

7:27pm, February 21, 2010 – Text from Elizabeth to Matt: I'm here without u baby but you're still on my lonely mind (corny band i know but i'm feeling the lyrics) ["Here Without You" by 3 Doors Down]

10:39pm, February 21, 2010 – Text from Elizabeth to Matt:

> your soul was made to inspire
> all my hidden desires
> your body fuels my fire
> your mind feeds my entire-ty
> 2-21-10 l*z xoxo

10:58pm, February 21, 2010 – Text from Matt to Elizabeth: Green eyes ill hold u near…cause ur the only

song i want 2 hear… love u sooo much baby!! Sweet
dreams!! ["Soul Meets Body" by Death Cab for Cutie]

**Sheila's Facebook to Elizabeth's Facebook February 21,
2010 11:00pm:** i'll love you forever, i'll like you for
always, as long as i'm living, my baby you'll be. sweet
dreams, and i hope the meeting tonight was a good one. :0)
<3

Elizabeth: hey ma you're corny as all hell but i don't know
what i'd do w/out u

**6:35pm, February 22, 2010 – Text from Matt to
Elizabeth:** Sorry i had 2 "fuck u" ur call, im in a mtng.
Why can't u b here w me rite now?!!

**6:36pm, February 22, 2010 – Text from Elizabeth to
Matt:** My wishes exactly

**10:01pm, February 22, 2010 – Text from Matt to
Elizabeth:** I'm gonna come c u within the next wk or wk
and a half and stay about 4 days! I can't wait 2 cu!! Its
gonna b like christmas morn.

**10:09pm, February 22, 2010 – Text from Elizabeth to
Matt:** U made my year, u r my only one – like give me
dates so i know when i need 2 have my own place

**10:17pm, February 22, 2010 – Text from Matt to
Elizabeth:** It's been so long since i've seen u…my lost
love! i've been so fuckin hollow since you've been gone!!

**10:37pm, February 22, 2010 – Text from Elizabeth to
Matt:** Gimme dates… i might b homeless 2nite

**10:44pm, February 22, 2010 – Text from Matt to
Elizabeth:** Wtf? just move in w/ me

11:03pm, February 22, 2010 – Text from Elizabeth to Matt: Call florida parole 4 me if u r serious… we need 2 b married 1st bfore they will approve it

11:08pm, February 22, 2010 – Text from Matt to Elizabeth: I told u i will fucking marry u anytime, anywhere!!!

11:26 pm, February 22, 2010 – Text from Elizabeth to Matt: Listening 2 "fade into u" – mazzy star. I meant i am through w/ all bs if i have the 1 person i was born 2 love 4ever

11:31 pm, February 22, 2010 – Text from Matt to Elizabeth: Then i will love u 4ever!!! Yes i know "fade into u" word 4 word

11:54 pm, February 22, 2010 – Text from Elizabeth to Matt: I'm counting the days until I can c ur face. sweet dreams of u if god answers my prayers

Text from Elizabeth to Austin, (whose house she was paroled to) February 23, 2010: Sorry i am such a disappointment… i warned u i'm crazy. i have been takin subs [Suboxone] and xanies [Xanax]

Elizabeth's Email to Sheila February 23, 2010 2:05pm

hey ma
i talked to [parole officer] and he talked to uncle ____
and i'll be living there from now on until i can get an apt of my own
love you gotta go

February 23, 2010

Things had gone well with Elizabeth living at Austin's house at first. They went to a bunch of concerts, which made Elizabeth extremely happy. After almost two weeks, Elizabeth and Austin had issues, probably her drug use. She had to leave Austin's. She moved in with her uncle, who lived in the same county (parole requirement).

Elizabeth's Facebook Post February 24, 2010:

a snowy day
my life is fading
from black to grey
hopefully one day
I will be able to say
I am glad
I performed well
In this tragic play

2:10pm, February 25, 2010 – Text from Matt to Elizabeth: Your love is an alternative universe far removed from the glossy façade of my empty life!!

2:20pm, February 25, 2010 – Text from Elizabeth to Matt: Love u 4ever, my tooth hurts bc of a nj dept of corrections filling. i am on my way 2 hospital – i have some poetic sweet nothings 4 u when I get there

2:49pm, February 25, 2010 – Text from Elizabeth to Matt:

Ur everything i've ever wanted
u r my deepest fears, & confronted
i desire ur presence
listening 2 evanescence
i fell in love w ur soul

w/out u i'm not whole.
ur kisses ur bites pulling hair
i want 2 b in ur bliss & only there
l*z xoxo

2:53pm, February 25, 2010 – Text from Matt to Elizabeth: Take their women…spend their gold…and leave their homes in flames!

3:16pm, February 25, 2010 – Text from Elizabeth to Matt: wtf, was this in response 2 my loving prose?

3:19pm, February 25, 2010 – Text from Matt to Elizabeth: No i'm actually wearing a shirt that says that.

3:27pm, February 25, 2010 – Text from Elizabeth to Matt:

true love
true blood
you're so rad
u make me wanna b bad
wanna rip off each other's clothes
but god only knows
what i'd b w/out you

3:45pm, February 25, 2010 – Text from Matt to Elizabeth: U have 2 do this 4 me…get on the computer and listen 2 the "shiny toy guns." the song is called "you are the one." the song is made 4 u and our relationship.

4:00pm, February 25, 2010 – Text from Elizabeth to Matt: the only song i know by them is "girls le disko"

4:03pm, February 25, 2010 – Text from Matt to Elizabeth: Listen to that fucking song rite now liz!!

Elizabeth's Text to Sheila February 27, 2010, 1:09pm:
call me this very second please…mother it is the weekend,
so u must return ur lil' girl's calls. Do it now… just had a
lovely conversation w/ my father and need u, and want 2
tell u how thankful i am 2 have u as my mommy

Elizabeth's Facebook Status February 27, 2010:
busy…gotta get cute…prepare for NA convention…gonna
get my groove on @ the convention center dance @
11:00pm…straightening up my uncle's house…at least I'm
freeeeeeeeeeeeeeeeeeeeeeeeeeeee

**7:35pm, February 27, 2010 – Text from Matt to
Elizabeth:** I bet u look like firecrackers on the 4th baby! u
better send me a picture! I miss u & love u 4ever!

**9:00pm, February 28, 2010– Text from Elizabeth to
Matt:** Major drama bc i went to na convention last night
and stayed at my girlfriend's house

**9:40pm, February 28, 2010 – Text from Matt to
Elizabeth:** Hey baby! I cant hear anything rite now i'm on
my way home from the sk8park listening 2 metal. R u ok?

Elizabeth's Facebook Status March 2, 2010: please God,
are you there?; it's me, Elizabeth

2:42 pm, March 2, 2010 – Text from Elizabeth to Matt"

   met w my p.o. at 10am
   I fucked up… positive 4 dope n thc…might get sent
back [to prison] friday
   I love u forever. please forgive me. i can't stop loving u

2:44pm, March 2, 2010– Text from Matt to Elizabeth: U
r a fuckin hot mess!!...but I will never stop loving u!

Undated Poem by Elizabeth

just call me Liz
I'm in the biz
another dopeless hope fiend
I pave the boulevard of broken dreams

March 2, 2010: Sheila's Journal

Elizabeth tested positive for opiates and thc today, no surprise. I later found out that she used urine from before the weekend, when she went on a total crack and heroin binge. So now Elizabeth is thinking when she gets tested Friday, there could be crack, heroin, and weed in her system – so she is trying to get a 'flush' or some way to cheat the test. I told her if they caught her, that might be worse than a positive UA, but she doesn't really care, she just does not want to go back to Bo Robinson [Prison Assessment Center]. Elizabeth said if she was sent back to Bo Robinson, she would do something to get sent back to prison – because in prison, you get time off for good behavior and she would get out sooner. She also said she may try to get into the psych ward of the local hospital she was in about a year ago, the Pines.

She says she is tired of this life and totally regrets her night of bingeing with Elicia, who is so mean to her and obnoxious – and I dislike her more than any of Elizabeth's drug friends. Bad things always happen when she is around Elizabeth, and Elizabeth said she is deleting her from her phone. Elizabeth has an appointment with her parole officer Friday morning, and he said she better test clean – to bring one set of clothes, and if she doesn't make the appointment, she better start running fast…

I guess the parole officer is giving her a second chance to have a negative test. He had already been to the parole center and knew she tested positive for opiates and weed.

168

He told her to take the NA One Day at a Time keychain off her bag, which bummed her out.

Parole Violated and Jail

Elizabeth's Voicemail to Sheila, March 4, 2010, 12:00pm

"Hey mommy it's me I'm home, I'm gonna be late for group [parole] today, some guy kind of like held me hostage at his house until just now, so I'm late...but I love you mommy"

Undated Poem by Elizabeth

16 hours
lethal sours
bound & gagged
teased w/bags

March 4, 2010 Afternoon

After she reported late to the parole center, her parole officer took Elizabeth to the county jail for parole violations.

March 15, 2010 The Ides of March Letter from County Jail

Mommy!

I finally heard from you! My first piece of mail! I've been trying to send you ESP messages… j/k…well kinda. I was hoping to get a longer letter from you! I've been

having a really rough time. Thank you for praying for me.
I've been praying as well. There are no visiting lists here,
you just show up: Sat & Sun 8:45AM to 8:45PM.

Despite my relapse, I felt like I was making progress. I
went to DRC [parole reporting center] instead of running.
But Daddy, [stepmom], & [stepbrother] saw me high at my
worst. I am so ashamed of myself & those images alone are
enough to keep me from picking up. The last night, when I
stayed out, I was just trying to get $ and the guy kept me
padlocked in his room for 16 hours. I did not want to stay
out all night, I was scared, he had a butcher knife &
wouldn't let me answer my phone.

I am disgusted with myself & I am taking a stand
against my addiction. New poem follows:

Heroin

it comes on swift
like the greatest gift
sets your mind adrift
 a ruse mends the rift
to innocent observers
only pleasure serves us
no family deserves this
but what could curb it?
what a plague I am
holding out my hand
iron will turns to sand
she's always on the lam
but not just from the cops
it's the unquenchable cyclops
her resistance it tops
she prays every day it stops
wishes she could go back 100 paces
her missteps she retraces
in her mind she sees the traces

172

of her families' horror filled faces

I don't know if they'll re-instate my parole or not. If I do go back to prison, Mom, I'm gonna need some $. Here I don't have even have a bra, shampoo or anything – but I'll be fine. In prison, I'll need at least basic personal hygiene items. At least if I did go to prison, I would get out sooner bc they take time off for good behavior & working.

Could you please get Matt's address & phone # for me & pass along my undying love? Tell Austin I'm sorry & grateful. I already wrote to my uncle. Oh & tell TJ I'm here, & that he can visit. To put $ on the phone you have to go to the inmate telephone website. I wish you lived closer so I could just live w/you & do it right this time. I miss you more than you know. Can you get the lyrics for "You Are the One" by Shiny Toy Guns. They only gave me 3 envelopes so I don't know if I'll be able to write back. Please, please, please get in touch w/ Matt, it will give me peace of mind. I pray for you, me & our family all the time. I'm sick of disappointing others, especially me. I love you, miss you, mean it! Send some pictures please!

Love, Your Little Lizzie
PS There is no library here at all!

March 30, 2010 Letter from County Jail

Hey Mommy!

You have no idea how happy I was to see you on Saturday! I talked to Daddy yesterday finally. He seems to think I belong in prison. I can't believe he actually put $ on the phone.

When I get out I want to be enrolled in school ASAP. I can't just be a lump, I need to save $ bc Riley will be 3 years old soon & I need him back in my life. I know everyone will be expecting me to fail, but I want to make everyone proud, especially Gram & Pop-pop.

Well I miss you so much more than you know! I can't wait to see you again! Thank you for making our time together special. I treasure those memories when I get lonely. I kinda wish I would have waived my hearing, but then you wouldn't have been able to visit.

Love, Your Little Lizzie
PS Tell Gram & Pop-pop I love them & I miss them!

April 1, 2010 Sheila's Journal

I had a good visit with Elizabeth on Saturday. She was in fairly good spirits, not blaming anyone, not complaining…. She is being her own lawyer on the parole violation charges. She may go back to prison, and she is okay with that. She is writing a lot of poetry.

Elizabeth asked me to text Matt and ask if she should wait for him/will he wait for her and his response was **"i will wait 4 liz 4ever!!"**

Undated Poem by Elizabeth

fare thee well
cold hard cell
cuz in my mind
new life I find
I dream of days
starring in plays
at Matt I gaze
and no more haze

April 7, 2010: Letter from County Jail

Hey Mama!

Well I just had my hearing. It was humiliating. Parole said "send her back." I'll be going back to EMCF [NJ state prison]. It should be next week sometime, so at least I'll be able to see you for one more visit. The hearing was nerve wracking but I'm glad it's over with and at least I'll be getting out of this hell-hole. When I get out of prison this time, I won't have to answer to anyone, I'll be able to leave this God-forsaken state. I talked to Daddy last night for a while. He thinks I should stay with you when I get out. He doesn't think I should be in New Jersey. Maybe I'll be out in time for the Super Bowl & we can have an "appetizer dinner," remember when we used to do that? Sorry this isn't very long. I love you, I miss you, & I can't wait to see you this weekend!

Love, Little Lizzie

New Jersey State Prison Two

Undated Poem by Elizabeth

the heavens raise hell
when this girl rings your bell
still livin' like this – I decree
bound once again for the penitentiary

**April 27, 2010: Letter: Sent back to Edna Mahan
Correctional Facility – Reception**

Dearest Mommy,

I was delighted and touched to receive the letter, card,
and money order. First of all I need to thank you for the
dinero [money] – it is a relief to know I will be able to
order the basics and I appreciate the work you did so that I
could be made comfortable in an uncomfortable situation.
Second of all, keep those letters coming; that kind of advice
is exactly what I need. I've read it 3 times already & I will
look at it more because it is inspiring.

It has been a humbling (or maybe humiliating is the
better word here) experience to say the least, walking
through these doors yet again. Every time someone
recognizes me and questions me as to why I'm back, I try
to remind myself that it is yet another consequence of my
actions, drilling home the point that I can't use successfully.
I am allergic to drugs. Something else that is key to my
sobriety is refusal skills. I've always had a hard time saying

"no" – whether it be drugs, sex etc. No matter how much I want to do the right thing, if I give into temptation, all the hopes & dreams in the world will not make up for my actions.

I'm not taking any psych meds, whatsoever. I will still see a therapist (if they can really be called that) once a month. I'm trying to spend most of my time either reading or playing Scrabble while in prison reception aka Boot Camp. I'm on my 3rd book. Unfortunately, since last year the selection has been severely depleted, but I managed to find *Beast* by Peter Benchley who wrote *Jaws, Border Music* by Robert James Waller & *September* by Rosamunde Pilcher, who wrote *Shell Seekers*. I kick ass in Scrabble. I play 6 times a day at least. There isn't much competition. Last game I got three 7 letter words in a row – a personal best.

I want to get this out ASAP. Can you give me Matt's # please? I miss you so much more than you know Mama! I'm so grateful to have support from you! Please tell me all about how it is up there in NY state. In DETAIL! I like hearing about simple things from the outside. I hope you are happy. Please send my love to Dad, [stepmom], [stepbrother], Gram, Pop-pop etc. Thank you in advance. I can't wait to hear from you again!

Love & Hugs, Your Little Lizzie

May 4, 2010: Letter from Edna Mahan – Grounds

My Dearest Mommy,

Well I finally got out of reception this evening, what a relief. It was so hot in there and the officers try to make you feel like 3rd class citizens. So I am in Alpha cottage AKA the Puppy Program. Unfortunately I don't have enough

178

time in to have a doggy, but I get to see the cute little labs every day.

There's a girl from my county here and she gave me a razor, some Q tips, a bar of soap, a cup & bowl, microwave popcorn, & a soda. Thank God for small favors. In the van on the way to the cottage I saw the officer from the cottage I was in last time & he smiled & waved.

In reception, I found *The Prince of Tides* (minus the first 35 pages) which I am halfway through & in the TV room here I found a Harlan Coben book: *Hold Tight.* I was so happy to get the books you sent today! Thank you so much Mommy! I'll probably have three books at a time going. I just want to read all the time.

5/5/10 Well my first day at work hasn't been so successful. They put me on grounds detail, which is mowing grass from 8am to 3pm w/ a break for lunch. Thanks to my lack of arm musculature, I'm having trouble w/ the pull start.

5/6/10 Well at least now I can start the mower but I've run into another problem… sunburn; I wear a hat so my face isn't burnt too bad, but my neck & arms are a horrendous shade of pink. OWWW! I am in so much pain but I'll have to go to work regardless. Sometimes we get to sit in the trailer attached to the officer's Gator (John Deere cart thingy) & ride around the grounds. Today I was about 100 yards away from the highway! It's fun because the detail officer doesn't always watch us; we're allowed to go more places than the other inmates.

5/7/10 We were mowing around the maintenance area this afternoon & all of a sudden I see a teeny tiny baby bunny! It was so cute. Then three more came out so another girl and I each caught one & moved them w/ their brother & sister so we wouldn't run them over. They were a little smaller than the size of my fist. So that was the highlight of my day.

Thank you so much for all the mail you've been sending! It makes me feel so good when I hear my name for mail call. I loved the article on Cupcake Brown – how inspiring. Also the "words to live by" article – when I get my own room I'm going to put it up on my wall so I can look at it every morning. Thank you for the $. I'm going to try to find a stamp from someone so I can send out your Mother's Day wishes. I don't have the supplies to make a card, but I want you to know that this weekend I'll be thinking of you & thanking God I was born to you. Even if I'm a brat sometimes to you, I couldn't be happier w/you as my mom.

What a gift it is to be able to tell your mom anything, & laugh and cry together & relate & enjoy the same things. I hope you have a joy filled day because you've more than earned it, Mommy. Thanks for being my supporter, confidante, shoulder, best friend, & mostly just for being you. Please pass "Happy Mother's Day" to Gram & [stepmom]. Please change my Facebook picture to the one where I have black hair. Thanks! I'm dying for some pictures to show my friends.

Oh you'll be happy to know I'm using one of the tools on the list you sent – "Alternatives to Behaviors" (No I'm not thinking about cutting). I've been visualizing being on the beach in Tulum, Mexico & imagining the feel of the sand on my feet, the salt air, etc. Very relaxing. It's almost 6 PM so I'm going on "the walk." From 6-8pm you can sign up to walk the loop & meet up w/ your friends from other cottages & talk.

Well no, I don't put much stock in a future w/ Matt. He's not very reliable. I believe we're soul mates, but that doesn't mean that he's the only one out there for me. When you get down to it, we are two extremely fucked up individuals.

Oh & I forgot to tell you that I said "No" to smoking weed while I was in the County Jail. Can you believe it?

5/9/10 Please continue w/the descriptions of your life & tell me what good food you're eating. I'm not watching what I eat. I figured I can do that now that I have such a physically demanding job. I saw the therapist yesterday, but she wasn't very helpful. I asked her to take me off the roster since I'm not on any meds & bc she seemed to be lacking in insight & in any constructive thoughts whatsoever – besides the occasional "mmm-hmm" or "uh-huh."

Of course today when I'm not outside working it's cloudy & it's sprinkling. I've got a Scrabble game & a Boggle game scheduled this evening. Remember how much fun we used to have playing Boggle? I haven't played in years. They have a movie channel where one movie is played on a loop throughout the day. Luckily, this is a very small cottage – nothing like max [maximum security] where you couldn't even hear the TV.

Oh – did you know this place used to be called Clinton Farms? It was a home for unwed mothers. Well 'A' cottage (mine) is next to the Chapel, away from the other cottages, which are all in close proximity. Behind the chapel, there is an old graveyard where little babies are buried; they all have the same small cross headstones. Edna Mahan herself is also buried there w/a larger marker.

Get this: I've got awful blisters on my feet from doing so much work in these darn boots & it is next to impossible to get a band aid in here. Apparently I have to order it on commissary! That's every two weeks.

I am making an effort not to curse as much as I have been in the habit of doing. I realize I need to start making new friends and I don't want to keep attracting the type that says "f***" every other word. Can you please send some perfume samples & some magazines, I feel as if I'm totally cut off from the fashion world. Muchas gracias! Well I'm going to send this out now, and I hope it reaches you quickly & finds you happy & healthy. You should take my

181

address off Facebook bc you're the only one I've gotten mail from so far – AT ALL. I miss you sooooo much. Lots of love, hugs, & warm fuzzy thoughts.

Love, your Bestest Girl (haha) Little Lizzie

May 18, 2010: Letter from Edna Mahan Correctional Facility

Dearest Mummy,

I finally received the pictures, note, & perfume samples. Thank you so much! I have the pic of me & my boy on my trunk so I can see it all the time. Oh! On Mother's Day guess what movie was playing… I forget the title but it's the one we always watched w/ Diane Keaton & baby Elizabeth w/ the apple sauce!!! It made me so happy to remember us sitting on our couch watching it. I finished reading *Sleep No More* by Greg Iles – very good, I lent it to my friend in another cottage & I am almost finished *Amy & Isabelle*, which is also one I can't put down. I got my commissary yesterday. I gave my friends a pack of cigs & a bag of coffee bc they didn't have anything & they were very grateful. Last night I cooked wraps for my roommate & me: spicy ground beef w/refried beans & cheese in a tortilla. Yummy!

Hola Mamacita! It's now Thursday afternoon, & I'm so excited bc this chick let me borrow her radio. It's the first I've heard rock music in about 3 months! What a beautiful thing to just chill & enjoy living in my little fantasy world in my head. On the other side of this paper I wrote songs I need to download whenever I get out from under DOC's thumb – or should I say DOC's long arm. Right now I'm listening to Eddie Vedder's cover of "You've Got To Hide Your Love Away." Thanx for the dinero. If you could please

182

send a tad more I would be very appreciative. I understand if you can't.

I'm probably going to Bo [Robinson] two Thursdays from today. Can you get me a disc-man PRETTY PLEASE, so I don't die of quality music deprivation @ Bo. I want to thank you for all you do for me. I don't take for granted all the help you've given me. Please tell me what's new in your neck of the woods. Oh, there's a guard here, so hot, that I heard had sex w/ Donna & he's been flirting w/ me. **Don't** write anything back about that.

I haven't written anyone but you yet – but then I haven't gotten mail either. It's depressing to come to terms w/the fact that I've ostracized myself so much from everyone that the only person who cares is my mama. I could fall off the face of the earth & it would make little or no impact. Woe is me, huh? I was just thinking about that time Kristen posted that thing about me belonging in prison…it makes me long for when I can leave the state whenever I want, have the option to smoke weed if I so choose, & look back at this period of my life & say, "Thank God I finally got my shit together." One can only hope.

The people I associate w/ here are pretty positive & we talk about what we're going to do differently & how much it sucks to deal w/the consequences & we don't tell war stories. I heard this Christian rock song earlier & it gave me goosebumps. I wrote down the lyrics, maybe you can google it, download, listen & understand what I'm talking about. I wish I could find a career that would be involved somehow w/ music. That's when I'm truly @ peace. I can't wait to have a road trip, & I can be DJ again. MISS YOU more than you know!

Is my writing too self-absorbed? I'm sorry if I'm selfish. I'm praying & asking God to remove my defects of character.

Love you a whole big bunch! Little Lizzie

PS "Desperately Wanting" by Better Than Ezra is on right now. Remember when we saw them w/ [stepmom] & Lauren?

May 20, 2010 Letter from Edna Mahan Correctional Facility

This too shall pass

I'm listening to "Telephone Line" by ELO. I'm feeling really disconnected and low. "I'm living in twilight" I think it says. I've tried to verbalize my feelings/fears in the hopes that would somehow lessen this fog that's clouding my mind. "I look into the sky – the love you need ain't gonna see you through." How did I manage to mess everything up? FUBAR. [Fucked Up Beyond All Recognition] I'm praying for redemption. What kind of mother abandons her son for a life of such degradation & desperation? Who have I become? How will I crawl out of this bottomless pit I've dug?

I can't imagine what Matthew M. [high school friend currently in prison w/ DUI] must be going through. I got a letter from him today. He sent pictures which made me happy. I don't want to write back until you send me some pics that I can send him. He talks mostly about God & is surprisingly positive. I feel like some lowly street urchin – his crime [DUI] was a mistake – it could happen to anyone. Mine was a collection of conscious decisions – a path I chose.

5/22/10 Well it's been 2 days since I wrote all that mess and I'm feeling a lil' bit better. I've been mowing hella grass. My arms & face are tan; of course the rest of me is practically translucent. My detail officer told me yesterday that he filled out my pre-parole packet. He had to evaluate me, talk about the kind of worker I am. He said he gave me an excellent report. They just played "My Own Worst

Enemy" by Lit. Remember when we met AJ Popov at that concert? I wonder what happened to my t-shirt that he signed. What picture did you send to Matthew M? He said Riley was beautiful. I still don't know what to write to him. His mom wrote me too, and said she'd like to take me to a Recovery group at her church. That actually sounds really good! I miss you bunches. Have a good Memorial Day.

Love & Hugs, Little Lizzie

Bo Robinson Prison Assessment and Treatment Center

Undated Poem by Elizabeth

Ode to Bo by L*Z

cut me a muthafuckin' break
cuz this is just about more than I can take
take another little piece of my heart
since I'm sure I'm already falling apart
kill me please
I'm on my knees
take my identity away
until I simply fade to gray

**June 10, 2010: Letter: Moved to Bo Robinson
Assessment & Treatment Center**

!Hola Mi Madre!

Como esta? I'm sorry I haven't written in a while. I've
been settling into my little corner of the 9th level of Hell. I
cannot believe it, but it has actually gotten worse here.
Getting those packages was such a relief. What would I do
without you Mama!? Thank you for getting everything to
me so quickly! I feel so much better about myself now that
I'm out of those prison khakis & have a lil' makeup on. I
absolutely love the bedding – it is comfy & cute. Thank
you, merci beaucoup, y gracias! Oh yeah & the dragonfly

socks were very thoughtful. Unfortunately I can only squeeze my fat ass into one pair of jeans, I must be like a size 9 now.

When you send me the cd player, can you pretty please get me Silversun Pickups' new album? They were nominated for a Grammy. Visits are MONDAYS from 7-9 but you need to be here at 6pm. I can't wait to give you a big hug Mommy! You have no idea!!! I agree w/ you that I should probably max out. As much as I want out ASAP, I know that being on parole is no picnic & I don't do well under supervision. By maxing out I'll probably get 18 more days taken off. So yes, I will take your advice and I want you to know that I <u>sincerely appreciate</u> your input.

I've been assigned to Ms. Boyle again. They stopped the distance learning classes so there really is little opportunity here to expand your mind. The library is supposed to be open <u>every day</u> but hasn't been open in <u>the week</u> that I've been here. I was watching Good Morning America & the weather guy was at Disneyland. It reminded me of our trip there & I'm sure we'll have more fun times @ Disney. Maybe now I won't be such a brat. (Well, we can always hope.) I'm sorry I get that way Mom, I really do treasure you & you don't deserve my wrath when I'm in a bad mood but thank you for accepting & loving me regardless. I'll write a longer letter tomorrow. Thank you for the stamps! Can you please send Sudoku & puzzles? I miss you, please write!

Love, Little Lizabuf

June 14, 2010: Letter from Bo Robinson

Hello my dearest Mommy,

I was so happy to be able to hear your voice today! I'm sorry if I was demanding but I only had 2 minutes. I can't wait until you come to visit! You have no idea. I've been thinking about where I should go after I get out: Florida, Colorado, California, Mexico, or even England. I can go anywhere since I'm maxing out. I'm trying to replay the last time when I got out on parole because as you know it was scary, disastrous, and not worth the trouble I've gotten in as a result.

Do you miss me? We need to have a movie marathon when I get out, starting with "Twilight – New Moon." I'm watching "Fatal Attraction" right now. It makes me realize that I've displayed some insane behaviors in relationships. (Not on Glenn Close's level). I don't want to be in a relationship until I'm secure in myself. I don't want to feel that someone "completes me." When I married Axel, I felt I had accomplished something – at least someone had chosen to be my partner & I could pretend to be grown-up.

I remember being @ Disney World, I think @ the Caribbean Beach Resort?? & laying on the bed eating my favorite cookies from that bakery on Main Street USA. I miss Disney. I think that's where I want to go first. Can we please tentatively plan on that? If you get me more books from Amazon, can you please get *Naked Lunch* by William S. Burroughs – he was a recovered addict back in the day, also *Snuff* by Chuck Palahniuk, & I've heard that Jennifer Armentrout is good. Right now I'm reading this lame thriller by Lisa Jackson & the library still hasn't been open since I got here. Can you pretty please send me the picture of me & Matt & the one with Riley in the bunny suit? How are Gram & Pop? And Jim & Debbie and Meg & fam? Who are you going to watch the fireworks with? Ok well I love you & miss you & can't wait to hear from you! Thank you for everything!

Love, Little Lizzie

June 17, 2010: Letter from Bo Robinson

Hey Mama!

It's that beat that makes you move, Mama. (Black Eyed Peas) Well it's Wednesday night & I just got out of my college prep class. I did well. Ms. Boyle gave us an Algebra packet– my favorite type of math. Oh! & I had my first chess class today. Ms. Boyle gave me a demerit yesterday for not having my notebook up to date. She had me sweep her office as punishment and we had a very good talk afterwards. Then in chess class, she called me & 2 other women into her office to give us some ICE CREAM! I had a little of 3 flavors: raspberry, butter pecan, & maple. Mmm! Just yesterday I was thinking how much I wanted some ice cream. Ask & you shall receive.

Well, I just received my packages. Thank you so much for the discman & CDs! The Muse CD is so good. Everything's better with music – don't you agree? I begged this girl to let me borrow her colored pencils so I could draw you some pictures as you requested. The sun is from the album cover of Sublime – "40oz to Freedom". I haven't gotten any mail from you for at least a week & this is like the 4th letter I've sent out to you. Please write more often. I like to know what's going on in your life. Can you please send my journals? Thank you! I want to start writing again. This evening I played Spelling Bee & won. Anyway, I won't write more, I want to get this out soon and just know I'm waiting on pins & needles for some mail.

Love you a whole bunch! Thanks again! XXOO Lil' Liz

June 28, 2010: Letter from Bo Robinson

Dearest Mommy,

Let me first start out by apologizing for behaving like a spoiled, whiny, brat [at visit]. I can't thank you enough for the sacrifices I know you've made in order to make my life a little bit more comfortable. I always feel like an asshole after I treat you like that. Please don't be hurt or mad. I really enjoyed being able to see you!! I miss you already! The visit went by entirely too fast. I think the whole bombshell about Axel getting remarried threw me for a loop.

Guess what happened as I was walking out of the visit? I looked on the ground & guess what I saw? Two $5s & a $10!!! OMG! So I bought a pack of cigs for $10. Don't write back about this. Please still bring some $ cuz this won't last long. I'll soon either be going to Fenwick, Kintock, or Columbus (prison halfway houses) for 30-60 days of mental health "treatment." TTYL.

Love, Lizzie

June 30, 2010: Letter from Bo Robinson

Mommy,

I'm still incredibly disappointed in myself for the way I treated you at visit. Especially when I get a letter from my father. He says he loves me but it hurts to come to terms with the fact that my whole family is ashamed of me & doesn't think I'll ever make anything of myself. New poem:

"I am ashamed of you"
A constant chorus
Fighting back tears
Sick w/ regret over wasted years
Sick of the taste of humble pie
Swallowing the lump to avoid the cry

191

Discouraging words that ring so true
Each day more aggravating factors I accrue
Dissecting my past turns my stomach to knots
This chance is my last, just one more shot

Hope you like my poem – just be aware that it's not my best. It was the first and only draft, I got frustrated & sick of it. Oh yeah, & our air conditioning is broken. It's like 90 something degrees. Everyone is miserable. No fans or anything. That's cruel & unusual punishment in my opinion.

I talked to this girl Anissa about Disney all morning. We talked about all the rides and about how, "it's fucking magical!" (Excuse my language but it was necessary for emphasis). I miss you! Please send everyone my love & hugs. <u>Sorry</u> I'm such a brat! With love, gratitude, & wishes for laughs & singing filled road trips,

Your Little Lizabuf

July 1, 2010: Letter from Bo Robinson

Dear Mama,

I just got your letter. I guess I expected it. I wouldn't want to visit me either after the way I acted. I was a selfish, ungrateful brat & I'm sorry I hurt you. I don't want to make excuses, I had no right to act the way that I did. I have everything I need & you've got me many additional things I wanted. I can't thank you enough for the comforts you've provided me w/. I really wish you would visit but I understand why you won't. I'm not going to ask for anything else but some pictures of Riley to get me through the next 8+ months.

Love, Elizabeth

PS I got my period (PMS) although I know it's no excuse.

July 21, 2010: Letter from Bo Robinson

Hi Mommy!

Well I'm writing this Wednesday night to let you know that tomorrow a.m. I'll be going to Columbus House in Newark. It's the place I told you they'd probably send me to, a prison halfway house with (supposedly) "treatment" for people w/ mental health issues. I'll do 3 months of treatment before I can go out & work. I almost got stuck here for 30 more days because last week my notebook wasn't up to date & the next day I got caught playing spades in someone else's room (we're not allowed to have/play cards or be in another person's room). Ms. Boyle punished me by not allowing to me to smoke for 5 days. I don't think I would've been able to stand another month here.

I'm kinda nervous about moving to this next phase only because it's uncomfortable going to a new place. I'm excited though. I've been a little down lately. I've kind of isolated myself the past week but I feel like you were right about this not being the place to find friends. I've been a bookworm which is always good "in my book" (ha) bc I'm expanding my mind while in here. I miss you so much & I'm sorry I haven't written. I love you so much Mama!

7/29/10 Hey Mama! I just got off the phone w/you, it was <u>so</u> good to hear your voice! Thanks for sending the package. Please know that what really gets me through is daydreaming about future happy memories at Disney, on the road again, & hopefully one day going on trips w/ Riley. I've had the urge to write which I haven't done in like 4 months. So let me know what you think. I wrote two poems about my divorce – I figure better to let it out & get it on paper than leave it bottled up, right?

the beauty of being unfettered
biography yet to be lettered
the ties that bind us together
fall away and float like a feather
my destiny will soon be revealed
these layers wait to be peeled

2nd poem about marriage/divorce:

from dizzying love
and flowering hope
to storm clouds above
stripped naked & broke
burn it all
so ashes remain
don't answer the call
release this pain
more gasoline
the past is a blaze
turn these nightmares to dreams
wake up from this daze
a secret smile
comes to the surface
walked a thousand miles
yes – I deserve this

Do you think I should be completely over the divorce by now? I know Axel is not tormented like I am, day in & day out – but maybe that's because he has what I want – Riley.

I love you! I miss you! I mean it! Love, Little Lizzie

Columbus House Prison Halfway House

August 5, 2010: Letter: Moved to Columbus House Prison Halfway House

Hey My Dearest Madre!

Well I just received the envelope you sent. Thank you for everything, especially the *People* mag & perfume samples. This place is something else. All we really do is sleep. I know that at least I'll catch up on my reading. I've already read *Memoirs of a Geisha* and *Sleeping Tiger* by Rosamunde Pilcher. Now I'm reading *Divine Evil* by Nora Roberts. Please send some books my way – as well as my journals – please, I really want them. Thank you again!

8/6/10 It's been a long week. We just had to move to the other ½ of the building bc they're putting the men on our side. It's awful bc the Kintock bitches are talking shit & saying we're crazy, blah, blah, blah. It's just a very negative vibe around here right now. It's messed up when we supposedly need treatment.

8/ 9/10 Hey, Mom, I just got your envelope with the *In Touch* magazine. Thanks for the stuff. I saw it was sent the 6th but you didn't put money in it. I don't know if you understand this or not but I don't have $ to do laundry, I don't have tampons & I just got my period and I am on the verge of tears and I need a fucking cigarette & I'm sick of being a bum. That's all I'll say about that. I don't want to be a brat but I needed to vent. I'm going to see if Jimmy G will give me some $.

Okay, well I just got up and went to the kitchen & watched a few minutes of "King of Queens," and it made me feel better. It reminded me of sitting on our couch w/ the blankets & pillows & eating pancakes & being silly. I'm sorry for being a big ball of stress. Well, I guess I'll be ending this, I really can't express how much I miss you, Mommy. I miss you & I hope you're doing well. Know that I'm thinking about you all the time. I wish we really did have ESP that would make this so much easier. I love you sooooooo much!

Love, your Lizabuf

August 26, 2010: Letter from Columbus House

Hey Mama!

I go for my initial parole hearing tomorrow. The hearing is at Northern State Prison. They drop us off, we have to wear jeans and a white collared shirt & they walk us through the men's prison to wherever we need to go. It's kind of good for a change of scenery & the guys are always hollering at us.

Hola Mamacita! Well it's Sunday morning & I just got off the phone w/ you. It's so nice to talk to you. I will be maxing out in either the end of February or the beginning of March because they are supposed to knock 9 days off for every month I spend here. Oh, I got a cran-grape juice from the vending machine – it reminds me of home.

Hi Mom! I just got off the phone w/you, it's like 7pm. You have no idea how much my mood is lifted talking to you, Ma. I was just thinking how lucky I am to have a mom, period – let alone one as understanding & supportive as you. You're down with good music & I can tell you

196

anything & even though you don't always like it, you don't make me feel like a piece of shit.

Thank you for once again sending a superior care package. The Ed Hardy notebook is so cute! And a wonderful selection of CDs, I must say. I can't stop listening to the Kings of Leon CD – every song is a masterpiece, I love the one about "dreaming of revelry" and track eleven where he says "Jesus don't love me, no one ever carried my load, I'm too young to feel this old." OMG – straight to my heart. I am so obsessed with Caleb Followill.

So this kid [at the men's prison halfway house next door] I've been writing gets out December 1st – he says he wants to come visit me. He's so cute & very sweet, considering he's been locked up from age 18 to 23. Don't worry, I'm not gonna marry the guy, but I do like him. I'm pretty sure he will look me up when he goes home. Can you see if he has pictures on Facebook pretty please. Joshua Y.

So I'm reading *Naked* by David Sedaris – so funny. Next is *The Talented Mr. Ripley*. Can you get me some info on Bonnaroo [annual 4 day music and arts festival held in Tennessee] please? I know you can't do everything & I'm grateful for what you <u>can</u> do. So, tomorrow, I'm going out with a group to do community service. Praise the Lord – I need to get out of this miserable building! I can't believe it hasn't even been 2 months. Alrighty Mama, I'm gonna sign off. I'll be waiting with bated breath for a letter of substance from you.

Xoxox Your Little Lizabuf

September 17, 2010: Letter from Columbus House

Hey Mama!

Thanks for the pictures. The ones of Riley brought tears to my eyes. Everyone said he's so beautiful. I loved the hair accessories – they're perfect. I loved everything! You send such good boxes! I can't believe you sent the picture of Josh – Thank you! He's a cutie, right? Anyway it's loony-toons as usual in here. Seven people got sent back to Clinton [prison] in the past week alone. I'm reading an Anita Shreve book right now. Oh, & I finished *19 Minutes* by Jodi Picoult last week. Please let me know what is going on w/ the family. Oh, & next time you send me a package, I will smoke Mavericks or Sonomas (menthol), they're cheap.

I just got the Twilight card tonight! It is perfect. Team Edward! Thank you for the stamps. I just sent 2 letters out tonight, one to Lauren & one to you. So Lauren sent me the sweetest card w/ a pic of two little girls giggling and it said, 'For always......that's how long we'll be friends.' It was so thoughtful. She enclosed a picture of her & Johnny @ his graduation – he's so tall!!!

OMG guess what just happened. Me & Jess got called for urines (everyone gets one once a week) & it was like 12:30am. We told the lady we didn't have to pee so she had us sit in the lobby. (You have to "void a specimen" within 2 hours or you go to directly to jail w/ out passing Go or collecting $200). So we're sitting being silly & in the front there are lockers where visitors can put their phones, etc. while they visit. So Jess is like "let's see what's in the empty ones". We found a whole Ziploc bag full of .... liquid crack! – just playing, coffee, which is like gold in this place. I smuggled it in my bra.

Mommy – listen it's Friday. Last night my friends & I took pictures in our underwear using a Nintendo DS – the staff allowed it in not realizing it had a camera. So some lady was using the game & hid it when a staff person came in. This was suspicious, so staff took it & saw the pictures. Three of us are on film in some state of undress. Not a sexual act, but I may get sent back to Bo [Robinson] when I see the disciplinary committee, because cameras aren't allowed. If I do I'm sorry. I'm so disappointed in myself because go figure, last night was the first time I got my picture taken. I love you & miss you & I hope you're not mad at me. I'm shaking & I feel like I'm gonna puke. I'm one of the ones that for the most part follows the rules.

Well it's Sunday night so obviously I didn't get sent back. My friend Erica got sent back bc it was her Nintendo DS. The rest of us will find out tomorrow what our punishment will be. So I may get a 4 x 4 x 4 which is 4 weeks extra duty (more chores), 4 weeks journaling every day, and 4 weeks loss of privileges (i.e. no store trips, no cashing money orders). So please pray that this all works out. And of course there's the fact that all of the staff have seen pictures of me in my underwear. Do you realize that at every facility I've been in (except the one where I was pregnant) I've gotten in trouble for something sexual? Anyway, I'm trying to keep my nose clean. I miss you & love you & I'm gonna try to call you as soon as I can.

Lots of Love, Little Lizzie
PS I just heard "Safety Dance"

September 30, 2010: Letter from Columbus House

Dear Mommy,

It's Wednesday night. I'm so fucking frustrated. I'll start at the beginning. Monday night the manager called me to the control booth to question me about the letters between Josh (the guy who writes me from the men's halfway house next door) & me. They searched all my stuff and took all my letters, but they also took my Alice in Wonderland notebook w/all my stamps.

199

So yesterday the director called me into her office and put me on a contract for 45 days. It cites "engaging in sexual behavior, having your picture taken, and fraternizing." I can't get in any more trouble until November 12th or I'll get sent back to prison. I've got 4 weeks restriction (can't go anywhere), 4 weeks journaling, 4 weeks extra chores & 4 essays due Fridays. So hopefully tomorrow in the mail I'll get the money order from Daddy to send you. I'll sign it so you can deposit it in your bank account & I need you to use it to buy me cigarettes. Please don't tell Daddy... he doesn't want the $ he sent to go to smokes. I need 4 packs of Newport 100's please. Of course I'm going to be on my best behavior from now on. At least I can still get visits. I miss you so much, you don't even know. I wish it was Thanksgiving already, I'm so lonely.

I'm sorry I screwed up so bad. You can bet I'm going to mind my p's & q's from now on. Please don't tell Daddy I got in trouble. He's already disappointed in me enough. I've been thinking that I should probably find some sort of sex addicts meeting for when I get out because a lot of the trouble I get into is related to sex. Can you see if you can find some info online for me?

Oh I just read *The Virgin Blue* by *The Girl w/ the Pearl Earring* author. It was good. Can you send one of my wedding photos please? I want to write about the emotions it evokes. I've got plenty of time to do journaling now. Hopefully my case manager will let me call you tomorrow. Thank you in advance! Love you!!

Little Lizabuf XOXO

October 4, 2010: Letter from Columbus House

Hey Mamacita!

Well first of all, thank you so much for my package. As always it was much appreciated. I finished *The Girl Who Played with Fire*, I couldn't put it down. I can't wait to read the last one. Lisbeth Salander is badass! So what I still need is razors, body wash, lotion, conditioner & of course CDs & mags. For CDs, I want Nirvana, Sheryl Crow, Zeppelin, INXS – do you still have the MTV Buzz CD w/ Cannonball? Oh! Do you have Big Head Todd & the Monsters?

So January 28th [Elizabeth's release date], can you believe it? I'm so excited to go on our road trip & listen & sing along to all sorts of music. That is just bliss; music, good company, anticipation of Disney, freedom, the beautiful scenery. Did you ever see "The Wall"? I watched it once when I was stoned w/ RJ & Mike – I'd like to watch it again.

I love you bunches. Thanks for being my best mommy! Why do I still act like a little kid sometimes? Will I ever grow out of that?

Love, Little Lizzie

October 6, 2010: Letter from Columbus House

Hey Mama!

Well I'm sorry I was so cranky when I spoke to you on Friday night. This place is just getting to me, especially the [lost] package thing.

I finished *Atonement*; it was an excellent book with a COMPLETELY bullshit ending. Now I've reduced myself to some Nicholas Spark mushy drivel, *The Guardian*, but I haven't started it yet, we'll see. I've got Henry James's *Portrait of a Lady* but haven't had the concentration for that.

I couldn't believe that my own Mommy managed to churn out an almost 8-page letter – there *were* a lot of spaces. But that is exactly what I've been needing. I've already read it 3 times.

OMG – I traded someone my CD player so I could listen to their radio for a few hours, and guess what's on? "<u>Just to win the love of a girl like you</u>"!

*Do you have Depeche Mode that you can send?

So the first 20 pages of Nicholas Sparks made me nauseous, so I'm starting a book from Oprah's Club, *The Story of Edgar Sawtelle*. It is a heavy tome, so it should keep me occupied for a while.

Oh, and Jess and I were talking about this last week. When you come to prison, you're forced to shower w/ other women, so it's like you start becoming critical about parts of your body that you never thought there was anything wrong with before. So as much as I try to be satisfied with what I've got, it's like you're under constant criticism, but at least I'm not puking – and I'm trying to get more disciplined with my fitness routine.

So now to respond to your letter. I'm really grateful that you're going to help me find someplace safe when I'm released. It really gives me a lot of peace of mind. I realize that the rest of my life is riding on the decisions I make on January 28th, 2011 [the day of her release].

Believe me, I am cognizant of the challenges facing me, I've been through this I don't even know how many times anymore. I do know that I'm sick of sitting in places filled with regret and longing. In all honesty though, even though there have been meetings that I've especially enjoyed & related to, I've always felt like a fake when I'm in the rooms [of AA and NA]. I'm always like, "Are they *really* deep down glad that they're not using?" Because I know that I still want to get high – I mean, it's one of my favorite things to do, obviously.

202

I've said this many times: I want to WANT TO stop getting high, but I don't think I've ever, since the first hit of weed, not wanted to. And then when I first did dope, it was like I had finally found what I had always been looking for. I could turn off my head and, just by taking some kind of chemical, I could change my mood & be the person I couldn't be without it.

All these consequences SHOULD make me never want touch anything again, but I'm just not there. Don't get me wrong: I don't want to pick up a crack pipe or a needle, but I feel like I'm not at my best or where I want to be without a joint or a pill.

I was talking to my friend Barbie and she was telling me her mom was addicted to Xanax but she has [a diagnosis]. Her pharmacist gives her a weekly supply so she won't be able to take too much. I think that's a viable solution; do you? I do want to eventually get to a place where I can say that I don't need ANY kind of substance for me to live comfortably in my own skin. I think that in an environment with people who are happy in sobriety, like the recovery community in Florida, I can eventually do it.

It's going to be a while before I have my shit together how I want. And I think that some kind of maintenance (benzos) will help me make it through those stressful times ahead. I do have a diagnosed Anxiety Disorder and it's always been hard for me in social situations, even when I was just five, just being around extended family. I feel like I would be setting myself up for failure [by aiming to be completely abstinent] because if I had nothing to help me cope, at the first uncomfortable moment, I would be out running the streets on a mission for a bag.

Maybe it's justification, I don't know, but I feel it'll give me better odds. You know how quickly I've picked up in the past upon release (on release day most times) & there's so much riding on this time. I don't want to crash & burn before I've given myself a chance. That's why I don't want to delay the Florida trip too long. Hopefully I'll be able to save some money from working here – but it's going to be hard – they take almost 50% of your paychecks.

I know that my sobriety has to be my number one priority. I really have to work on calling someone when I feel like getting high, because honestly, when I get that mindset, the last thing I want to do is tell on myself & prevent it from going down. I'm going to have to find a sponsor that I really connect w/ bc the few times I've actually had one, I didn't really use them.

I know there is so much riding on this chance as far as family is concerned. But – not to be ungrateful – a letter every now and then and sending stuff once isn't really a strong support system. Not that I'm saying I don't deserve everything I get as far as distance.

But when I am released, I really have no other choice but to sell my ass at first because they don't give General Assistance to people with drug charges. If I didn't have you as my support, I don't know what I'd do.

Alright, I've been serious long enough. I just heard a version of "Stairway to Heaven" w/ the lyrics to Gilligan's Island. It's called "Stairway to Gilligan's Island."

*Before I forget – what's that song I think I told you is my bar theme song by Finger 11?? It's driving me crazy! Please help, lyrics if possible.

I've spent the day reading the 2010 Birnbaum Guide to Disney World [where we planned to go on the drive to South Florida]. Tomorrow I'm sitting down with Anissa to go over the itinerary. I miss you and love you! Hope to talk to you soon!

xxxo! Little Lizabuf

October 14, 2010: Letter from Columbus House

Dear Mommy,

So there's a whole bunch of drama going on here, did I tell you how a few weeks ago, two people got sent back [to prison] for stealing a money order? Evidently one of those girls was involved with one of the case managers named Miss B.A. Well after it was revealed about the $, some other girl said Miss B.A. was holding her $ [money order] & wouldn't give it back. She apparently went on vacay w/ the chick's $. So the girl filed a police report, the counselor was apparently led away in handcuffs. There was a rumor she was also charged w/ sexual assault.

So this place is the sorriest excuse for a halfway house. Oh, & when you work, you have to give them 33% of your check for house fees and 17% to DOC [Department of Corrections] for fines! That's why I need to be a waitress so they won't be able to touch my tips. Daddy was like, "Don't you guys go out in pairs or something?" He's worried about the fact that I'm in the inner city & I'm white, which is certainly valid. He was like, "They worry so much about who comes to visit you & what gets sent to you, but what about your safety when you go out?" I hadn't given it much thought, but it is down the street from some projects and a big park. It's not as if I can carry mace or something, I'll just have to work on my stance of being unapproachable... yeah right, everyone always says how innocent I look.

Axel did teach me some self-defense stuff, where I act like I'm afraid, back up, put my hands up, and then go in & push my thumbs in their eyes & knee them in the crotch. But honestly, I've been in some of the worst projects in Atlantic City, Camden, and even Florida. I was in West Palm Beach & and I was wearing a mini-skirt & halter top & nobody messed with me.

I just got the package you sent! Thank you soooo much Mommy! It was totally unexpected! I love the deodorant! And the much-needed tampons. I love all the pictures of

205

Riley – he is so freakin' handsome isn't he?!? I wish you would send some pictures of yourself Sheila Beila!

Oh & I need more stamps ASAP. Did I tell you I wrote Gram & Pop & drew a goldfinch for them? I liked the article you sent on Elin Nordegren, I guess I need to see how it feels to be the one that is cheated on. I'm just looking at how my handwriting gets progressively sloppier as my writing goes on. It's just when I have a lot to say I can't write fast enough.

Oh, did I tell you I went to community service? Well, we go to this Goodwill place in Newark where there are homeless men living & we talk to the old lady reverend and some other ladies. They give us coffee & pastries, then we talk, then we go up to the store & grab any trial-size toiletries we need, then we had Subway, mmmmm yum-gubbies it was roast beef on honey oat bread, w/lettuce, banana peppers, jalapeno peppers, oil, vinegar, salt, pep, & mayo, it was bangin'… they also gave us these pepper relish chips which were surprisingly scrumptious, and I had cherry coke. Then for dessert…Louisiana crunch cake by Entenmanns – it took all my will-power not to eat more than one slice. Oh, I completed a nutrition course & for the last day the facilitator brought us smoothies & mango slices. Aaah – the simple pleasures.

I'm going to Northern State Prison tomorrow, to see the Dr. A boy there wants to write me – Jose P. Will you print out his DOC sheet for me pretty please. I might not write him but he's so sexy, I just want to have a pic of him.

I'm going to send Riley a Halloween card next week. I'm looking forward to another long letter! Oh! and I abso-fucking-lutely LOVE Arcade Fire!! Their new song "Ready to Start" is phenomenal! OMFG – just got a letter from none other than Bob!!!!! Didn't see that one coming! So he was really sweet, says he'll always love me, etc. Can you send his # por favor? Muchas gracias por las cosas, uno mas vez madre. I love you big bunches!

Love, Lizabuf

October 25, 2010: Letter from Columbus House

Dear Mommy,

Well I got 3 cards from you this evening. Thank you. I just finished *Edgar Sawtelle,* a tragic ending. Now I'm reading *A Deadly Game* about Laci Peterson.

Today in NA, I shared a condensed, highly censored version of my story. It went ok. I was asked & even though I didn't want to, I did it because I'm gonna need to start sharing. I'm a little pissed off @ this lady Joanne bc I tell her stuff cuz she's from my county…I've talked to her about how I want to smoke weed, & she put me on blast (as they say here) & I feel betrayed.

Anyway, I called my friend from next door (DOC men's halfway house) who I got in trouble for writing and guess what – he got in <u>absolutely</u> no trouble at all. Double-standard bullshit. Even though what they caught was a letter from HIM to ME!?!! Of course I can't make a fuss about it, because we're not supposed to correspond (don't worry I haven't written) but he has a cell phone & when we were @ rec he held the # up on a piece of paper. He's leaving on Dec. 1st and I need him to help me out w/ $ when he goes home. Oh & he's supposed to send me phone cards this week. I'm also writing this guy from the state prison we go to when we need to see the Dr. His name is Dan and he's <u>really</u> smart & funny.

Love, Lizabuf

October 31, 2010: Letter from Columbus House Prison Halfway House

Happy Halloween Mommy!

Well, as you can imagine, my favorite holiday sucks right now, although I am wearing my vampire socks. There was a Halloween Party (I don't think you can even really call it a party) for families on Friday night, we got a bag of chips & a fucking Capri Sun, while the kids all got bags of candy, which I think is bullshit, because the kids can go out & get their own candy, right?

Oh, I should be able to go out to look for work on November 8th, if everything goes as planned. Can you please send me some purses?

I hope the new med works out, are you off the Seroquel? I hope so bc the long term effects are uncontrollable facial tics.

It's funny that you think I have good insight, because that was one of the reasons cited when parole gave me a hit, "lack of insight into criminal behavior" or some bullshit.

Right now I'm reading *A Piece of Cake* by Cupcake Brown, remember you sent me that article about her? It's 11:30 lights out so I gotta go, but I love you & hopefully I will be able to call you this week. I hope the meds are working. I love you soooooo much! & I miss you more!

Love, Little Lizzie

November 7, 2010: Letter from Columbus House

Hello my bestest Mommy!

It was so nice to finally talk to you! I'm sittin' here listening to my friend's radio, I'm so pissed, they're giving

208

out tickets for Kings of Leon & a tailgate party pre-show. B-O-O-H-O-O!! Oh well, I'm sure they'll be still touring when I get out. I fucking <u>LOVE</u> them; especially my future husband, Caleb. I hear he's a drunk.

I'm reminding myself of all the concerts I went to w/ Austin & if I stay away from coke & dope, I'll be able to go to shows all the time!!!! Another incentive I'm giving myself is tattoos. I can't wait to get one when I get out as a celebration of my freedom.

Things to Remember

I'm deaf to what these people
say about me
I've got a lot to learn
that's why I'm here
I came here by myself
I'm leaving by myself
this is just a chapter
in my life story
not my whole life

Ooh, "Gone Away" by The Offspring, wasn't that concert amazing? I cannot wait until we're driving down to Florida and playing the radio or those old WDOX tapes and singing along. I <u>think</u> I'll even stop complaining about your singing because I'll be so happy. There's people here that annoy me <u>way</u> more than you can, and I have to bite my tongue . I'm so happy that my counselor said she sees a change in me. I really am trying, even though I have reservations, I always make sure to share & pray for God to take away the obsession to use.

Lil' Wayne just got outta jail yesterday. I'm sure he's having the party of a lifetime down in Miami! Damn, TJ has 3 yrs. clean now, remember when he had only 9 mos? I wonder if Matt's really gonna stay clean. He & I are both chronic relapsers. But while he's clean, he really seems like he's got good recovery, good support, but I've never been around him when he's fallen – well, I talked to him on the phone in Moab when he was all fucked up. I hope we can work out…

Well I want to send this out. I love you & miss you! Love, Lizabuf

November 12, 2010: Letter from Columbus House

MOMMY!

OMG OMG OMG!! I absolutely positively am in love with the bag you got me! It is the cutest little thing, I was so happy when I got it! And I'm so excited to use it, I can't wait! And thank you so much for the cigarettes, they were a surprise! I really appreciate it; I was on my last pack. I wish I could call you but, alas, I'm broke.

So let me tell you about my first day at work yesterday. At 2pm, we left. (I'm borrowing someone's black pants for now). We take 2 buses and finally get to Millburn. So the diner is pretty nice as far as diners go. There are so many desserts & pastries, OMFG – I'm drooling just thinking about it. Pies, huge cookies, carrot cake, oh & cheesecakes, right now there is pumpkin cheesecake…and what I want to eat the next time I'm there…chocolate covered cheesecake.

So I followed this girl Laura, basically shadowing her the entire night. At 10pm she left. I picked up one table w/ 2 old folks. The bill was $20 & they left me $4, so I was able to make the train fare home. Oh & after 8pm we're allowed to order, so I got chicken quesadillas, mmm… It was so good to eat real cheese & NOT processed chicken, and miracle of miracles – sour cream! Yummy! And I drank yummy coffee all night & cranberry juice. So Jean & I took the train back because the buses don't run that late, we left

@ 11:37 & didn't get back till 2am. It was rainy & windy & we had to wait for the 2nd bus forever. When we finally got back my feet were <u>killing</u> me. I need to get some good shoes. I got searched & took an ibuprofen, washed my face & brushed my teeth, got in bed & thanked God for my exciting day. It was so much fun. Please pray for me that I get some more hours. Well I love you & I miss you, oh, when you go home, if you go to Daddy's, please get me my black pants, (I have like 3 pairs), my black Kenneth Cole jacket, and anything else you see, i.e. shoes, shirts, & hats.

XOXO Elizabeth

November 14, 2010: Letter from Columbus House

Hey Mommy!

It's Thursday afternoon and I just got off the phone with you. I want to apologize if I was being a brat. It's no excuse but I'm really frustrated about this work situation.

I'm sorry I hurt your feelings when referring to you as crazy – I'll stop. It's not fair and I wouldn't want you to say that about me.

I know I care too much about what other people think (well, when I'm sober). My counselor said I was acting like a spoiled brat and it made me cry. She said you don't owe me anything and I'm an adult. She's right. I'm sorry. I don't want to take you for granted. I'm lucky to even have a mom, let alone one as understanding and generous as you.

You're my best friend and I don't know what kind of person I'd be without you. I only hope that I make you happy too, Mama. I love that I can tell you anything w/out feeling you'll reject me. Maybe I do rely on you too much. I'll try to be more independent, but sometimes I still feel like a little girl. I'm going to try to be more considerate & stop letting little things bother me. I tear up when I think

211

about you picking me up after not seeing you for so long. It's going to be great!

I think Juan, the chef at the diner, likes me. He kept smiling @ me. He yelled @ the one girl Laura & she yelled back. But I'm not really confrontational like that so I should be fine.

I love you & I miss you & I will be anxiously awaiting a letter whenever you feel up to it!

Love, Lizabuf

January 18, 2011: Letter from Columbus House

Hey Mommy! I miss you & love you! Only 10 Days! OMFG!

"What are u gonna do when you get outta Columbus/ Kintock, Liz?

Liz, "I'm going to Disney World, bitches!"

Love, your little Lizabuf

Freedom!!

Undated Poem by Elizabeth

> an everlasting well
> of energy
> waiting to be dispelled
> from inside of me
> every nerve ending
> stands at attention
> jumping, dancing
> craving only redemption
> buried inside
> this cool, calm shell
> yearning to break out
> magic visions to sell

January 28, 2011: Freedom

I picked up Elizabeth at Columbus House. She had maxed out – no more NJ Department of Corrections/NJ Parole controlling her. We stopped at a North Jersey mall so I could meet her friend Robert, an older gentleman who had frequented the diner where Elizabeth had waitressed while in the prison halfway house.

Elizabeth's Facebook Status January 28, 2011: freedom is just another word for nothin' left to lose ["Me and Bobby McGee," Janis Joplin]

Elizabeth's Facebook Status January 30, 2011: @ the waterpark: fayb!

Leaving New Jersey

When we left New Jersey, we drove down to visit my brother and sister-in-law in South Carolina. Then we drove to Palm Beach County, Florida. Elizabeth had gone to two rehabs there & she felt it would have a good recovery community. We found a residential motel in West Palm Beach & we talked to a young guy who was doing repairs to various units. Elizabeth paid the first week's rent. The next day we went to Delray Beach. It was great – it had been so long since we had gone to the beach together. The next morning I drove home. The guy at the motel (Marc) was soon Elizabeth's boyfriend.

Elizabeth and I talked on the phone every few days. Elizabeth had gone to rehab five times. She had been locked up in either jails or state prison for three years. Elizabeth had tried to make changes numerous times. She was 26 years old. I wanted a close relationship with her. I didn't nag her or question her about her substance use. When we talked on the phone, we talked about family, friends, music, books, food, movies… But if she didn't call me within 3 days, I would be freaking out. I would call and text. Then I would text and call, over & over – but she always eventually called to tell me she was okay.

Elizabeth's Facebook Status February 23, 2011: loving life

Elizabeth's Facebook Status February 24, 2011: needs a massage

Elizabeth's Facebook Status March 4, 2011: watching fast times @ ridgemont high i love jeff spiccoli

Elizabeth's Facebook Status March 10, 2011: "I have woven a parachute out of everything broken." –William Stafford

Elizabeth's Facebook Status March 14, 2011: "even on a cloudy day..i'll keep my eyes fixed on the sun"– cage the elephant, "shake me down"

Elizabeth's Facebook Status March 21, 2011: Watching Anthony Bourdain no reservations – i wanna be a billionaire so freakin' bad – so i can be in french polynesia – it brought me back to the simplicity i enjoyed in mahahual, mexico

Elizabeth's Facebook Status March 22, 2011: I might be bad but I'm perfectly good at it

Elizabeth's Facebook Status March 23, 2011: Enraptured by radiohead video – lotus flower "you float like a feather in a beautiful world"

Sheila's Facebook Reply/Comment to above lyric: "what the hell am i doing here? i don't belong here"

Elizabeth's Facebook Status March 26, 2011: Mark from Philly says, "rules are made to be broken." then it must be true.

Elizabeth's Voicemail to Sheila March 27, 2011

(crying) Mom I just broke up with Marc and I just feel like the worst fucking piece of shit in the world and I fucking did it again…I'm fucking awful and I just don't know what to do…and I just wanna fucking throw up…because I'm fucking never going to change…I'm never going to change…Mommy just call me back – please soon, please just call me back

Undated Poem by Elizabeth

I'm like a comet
I light up the sky
maybe you'll vomit
& surely you'll cry

Marc and Elizabeth

Marc and Elizabeth stayed friendly. He worried about her and continued to try to help her.

Elizabeth's Facebook Status April 19, 2011: my next tat: TRUST NO ONE

Elizabeth at JFK Medical Center July 20, 2011

Elizabeth called me from the hospital. She had a blood infection. Liz said the pain was so bad she was screaming and someone called an ambulance. I flew down to Florida for several days, soon she was released. Liz, Marc, and I went out to dinner. The next day I flew home.

Elizabeth's Facebook Status December 4, 2011: i'm listening to "Fall For Your Type" by Jamie Fox on Pandora

Elizabeth's Facebook Status December 24, 2011: i'm listening to "zero" by the yeah yeah yeahs on Peaches Radio by Pandora

Elizabeth's Facebook Status December 31, 2011: i'm listening to "Bill Gates" by Lil' Wayne on Pandora

Elizabeth's Facebook Status January 11, 2012: i'm listening to "Forty Six & 2" by Tool on Pandora

Elizabeth's Facebook Status January 19, 2012:

………only a cold, still life………
"Angel in the Snow" – Elliott Smith

Elizabeth's Facebook Status March 14, 2012:

Thank you God, for today and every day.
Ice Cube – "Today Was A Good Day"

Sixth Rehab and Palm Beach County Florida Jail

In April 2012, Elizabeth got two drug charges. She was arrested and taken to Palm Beach County Jail. I paid her $200 bail. Elizabeth asked her grandparents if she could borrow money for rehab and they agreed. She went back to C.A.R.E., a Florida rehab she had attended in 2006.

June 8, 2012: Letter from Elizabeth to Gram & Pop-pop from C.A.R.E. Rehab, Florida

Hi Mom & Gram & Pop-pop!

It was nice to talk to you this morning. I've been making good use of my time here. Since I've been here before, I have the advantage of knowing which aspects of the program to use to the fullest. I get the biggest benefits from yoga, psychodrama, NA meetings, and individual counseling with my therapist, Craig. As I spoke to you about last week, I would like to go to a halfway house to continue living in a somewhat structured environment. My counselor & I agree that in my early recovery, that will be the safest option. I plan to seek employment as soon as I get to the halfway house. The halfway house I want to go to is called Freedom House. It is in Palm Beach Gardens, and as we talked about, it is $700 to move in, which includes the 1st two weeks of rent but not groceries. There are several restaurants in the area so hopefully I will be able to get a job quickly. I hope all is well in NJ! Thank you again!

219

Love, Elizabeth

July 2012: Elizabeth Completes Rehab

Soon after **Elizabeth completed rehab in July 2012,** she started using again. When she met a new boyfriend, she soon moved in with him in North Palm Beach.

Elizabeth spent 30 days in the Palm Beach County Florida jail in September/October 2012.

September 26, 2012: Palm Beach County Jail

Mood: bored as hell & I wanna get ill Song: Boyz in the Hood
Artist: Dynamite Hack

Hey Mama!

Well I borrowed my friend's colored pencils so there's your Disney World drawing (sorry it's lame but that's as much detail as I could come up with for Cinderella's Castle w/o looking at it). There's a song by Tupac & the hook goes… "Ain't got time for bitches, gotta keep my mind on my mutha****in' riches." Anyway, as you can imagine, in here I use that as my theme song b/c when you're in browns (what trustees wear) you can't afford to get in a fight, or you will lose the credit you've earned (one day for every <u>six</u> worked). It's insane the amount of work you have to do to earn one day of freedom. And the $$ the PBSO [Palm Beach County Sheriff's Office] saves by having us work… after dinner, about 15 of us girls go down to the kitchen to clean. I'm getting blisters on my hands from putting away probably 1,000 steaming hot trays. If they would let us listen to the radio while we worked it would be more tolerable. I never really get to hear music. But I'm super psyched because tomorrow I'm off and for the past 2 Thursdays I've been watching "Glee" & I <u>LOVE</u> IT! Last week was "Britney 2.0" & all the songs were by Brit. The show is so funny, I highly recommend it! I hope work is going well. I'm glad Gram had a good party. Send my love & big hugs & smiles!!!! Robert wants me to come to New Jersey. He said he looked up Axel & says "he was a bad person." Lol, duh. I love you & miss you!

xoxo, Elizabeth

Visit to New Jersey

Elizabeth's Voicemail to Sheila August 2012

"Happy birthday to you, happy birthday to you, happy birthday dear mommy, happy birthday to you!

Happy birthday, I love you, I'll talk to you at length a la manana, muah, happy birthday, love you, miss you, big hugs, big kisses, bye"

December 2012

Elizabeth wanted to come back to New Jersey for a visit. Since she had no photo ID, she couldn't fly or take a train. The bus ride was three days long. I flew down to Florida and rented a car. I met Elizabeth at her friend Marc's. She went to Western Union to get money from her New Jersey friend Robert, who was paying for us to stop at Disney World on our long drive to New Jersey. When we arrived at the Disney World Resort, Elizabeth slept most of the day and went out at night. The second night, I persuaded her to come with me to the Magic Kingdom. The main thing I remember is that there was a Radio Disney Dance Party, and Elizabeth joined in.

It was an okay visit. Elizabeth was using, and I was stressed – but she got to see many friends and family members.

We went to our church one Sunday. Elizabeth got a lot of hugs. She was very happy to be back at the church where her bff's dad was the minister, where she was confirmed, and where people were so obviously delighted to see her. Elizabeth recorded part of the church service on her phone.

On December 19th, five days before she headed back to Florida, Elizabeth and I went to the mall – Macy's specifically. Elizabeth fell in love with a Hello Kitty purse and I bought it for her as a Christmas present. As we walked past the displays, I saw earrings I really liked for $24. I asked Elizabeth if she would buy them for me for Christmas. I could see her hesitate a fraction of a second. That gift would cut into $ earmarked for drugs. Elizabeth bought the earrings for me. I've kept them – along with her dated receipt, to remind me of the choice she made that day.

On Christmas Eve, Elizabeth took the bus back to Florida. Grammy and pop-pop met us at the Atlantic City bus station to say good-bye.

2013 – 2014 Endocarditis

Elizabeth's Last Facebook Status was on January 23, 2013: Love "A new command I give you: Love one another. As I have loved you, so must you love one another." –John 13:34

December 2013: Hospital, West Palm Beach, Florida

One day in December of 2013, Elizabeth called me and said she was in the hospital. It was life threatening. She had endocarditis.

Endocarditis is a bacterial infection that people who inject drugs can get if they reuse/share needles, if their "works" are dirty, if their skin has bacteria on it, if they use unsanitary water when injecting, etc. This bacterial infection can travel to the heart and destroy the heart valves. It can be fatal.

My Dad and I flew to Florida. When we got to the hospital, Elizabeth was in Cardiac ICU. She was really skinny. She needed open heart surgery to replace a heart valve, but due to her low body weight, she was not strong enough for the surgery. She also needed six weeks of IV antibiotics. The plan was to have her gain weight to be strong enough for the surgery while getting the IV antibiotics. Elizabeth had used heroin and other opioids for years – she was currently using Dilaudid she bought on the streets. Dilaudid also happened to be the painkiller the hospital doctors kept her on – first for the pain of the endocarditis, then for the painful open heart surgery. They gave her Dilaudid in her IV every 3 or 4 hours.

Elizabeth was getting free legal drugs, she was encouraged to order whatever food she wanted, and her friend Robert sent her a brand-new smart phone. She was being taken care of and she had a place to sleep. The hospital had free WiFi. This was one of the happiest times in the last years of Elizabeth's life – for her and for her family. She called her son Riley every day. She talked to her dad most days and she called me 3 or 4 times a day. It was wonderful.

There was a hospital resident who often came to Elizabeth's room. Elizabeth really looked forward to her visits. The resident, her physician, and the cardiac surgeon – they all told Elizabeth that if she did not stop injecting, the next time she was brought to a hospital, she would be dead. But the hospital would not address treatment for Elizabeth's opioid use disorder. They told me they "didn't do that."

At 6:30 AM on the day before Elizabeth's birthday, Elizabeth's pop-pop and I were there as Elizabeth was wheeled into surgery with the hospital's head cardiac surgeon. Naturally she was nervous, as we were. We sat in the waiting area. Our flight home was that afternoon. The cardiac surgeon came out and told us she had come through surgery in good shape. He had not replaced her heart valve, but he had removed some growths from her heart.

After six weeks of IV antibiotics, Elizabeth was discharged. The hospital had kept Elizabeth on IV Dilaudid (an opioid) every 3-4 hours for her entire six week stay, so she started withdrawing a few hours after being discharged. Elizabeth told me she started shooting up again that day.

Elizabeth contracted endocarditis again and didn't get treatment. On Thursday April 3, 2014, Elizabeth called, and we chatted. She didn't mention anything was wrong. The next day, Friday April 4, 2014, around noon, a nurse called and told me Elizabeth was in the ER at a West Palm Beach hospital and her blood work was "incompatible with life." A few hours later, a doctor called and said that Elizabeth would not survive. He told me he couldn't imagine how she had managed to walk into the hospital unassisted. Elizabeth was "unconscious but comfortable." Late that night, at around 1:15 a.m. Saturday April 5, 2014, a nurse called and told me that Elizabeth had just died. She was 29 years old.

Her official cause of death was:

- Severe Sepsis
- Endocarditis from IV drug use
- Respiratory Failure
- Renal Failure

Undated Poem by Elizabeth

just when I'm feeling like gum on the bottom
 of someone's shoe
an angel swoops down & blesses me anew
this stranger across the aisle
has helped me walk just one more mile
she knows not what she's done for me
maybe it was simply out of pity
but even so, I'll take what was so freely given
in the hope that they just might let me into heaven

Words for Elizabeth

Elizabeth's Eulogy by her Aunt Meghan

I'm going to try to be brief so that I can get through this.

I think of Elizabeth and words don't come easily. I know that I have a swirl of powerful emotions and a huge love for the beautiful bright spirit that was my niece.

I cherish the memories of the adorable spunky little girl. Watching her grow from a precious baby to a precocious toddler, to a curious child, to a talented student, musician and dancer, a really smart, ambitious kid with a passion for music, animals and the world around her – she had a sense of adventure and of responsibility – though maybe not of purpose. She had incredible inherent artistic talents, deep compassion, a sense of humor and of dignity. All of this on top of being blessed with an amazing natural beauty, poise and light.

Why couldn't she find a path to happiness and health with all of that going for her? I'm guessing that this is the question on all of our minds – and I don't think any of us has an answer to it.

When I was putting the slideshow together it was tough to see her nearly angelic face in so many loving situations. So many family members and friends who loved her dearly and gave everything that they knew to give.

We're here today to celebrate her life and to try to find some meaning, or at least closure, for her loss. No one will ever know the depth of her demons, her illness, her darkness or understand her choices. I hope that through the memory of Elizabeth, each of us can find a bit more compassion for our family and friends in pain. Perhaps one day addiction and mental illness will have failsafe cures. I'm so sorry that I didn't know how to make a meaningful difference in her life.

For now, I hope to keep Elizabeth's spirit alive in me, remember the smiles, laughs, memories and love that she brought into our lives and try to channel the wonderful parts of her spirit for Good. I hope all of you will take an image of her light with you when you go.

Epilogue

For quite a while, I felt stuck as to how to best share and explain what I had come to understand in the years after Elizabeth's death. I wasn't a researcher, journalist, or writer. I knew if I attempted to write, in my own words, I would certainly fail to accurately convey the knowledge, science, ideas, and research that I wanted to. I believed any attempt on my part to discuss these various issues would inevitably lose a lot in translation. So I decided to quote the experts.

My understanding of the failed war on drugs, drug use, addiction, treatment, and mass incarceration began to evolve several years after Elizabeth's death. Ethan Nadelmann, founder and past executive director of the Drug Policy Alliance, really opened my eyes to reality when in 2016, I happened to watch his 2014 TEDTalk, "Why We Need to End the War on Drugs" on YouTube (TED, 2014). Portions follow:

What has the War on Drugs done to the world? Look at the murder and mayhem in Mexico, Central America, so many other parts of the planet, the global black market estimated at 300 billion dollars a year. Prisons packed in the United States and elsewhere. Police and military drawn into an unwinnable war that violates basic rights, and ordinary citizens just hope they don't get caught in the crossfire. And meanwhile, more people using more drugs than ever. ...

Which is why it's particularly galling to me as an American that we've been the driving force behind this global drug war. Ask...why the U.N. drug treaties emphasize criminalization over health, even why most of the money worldwide for dealing with drug abuse goes not to helping agencies but those that punish, and you'll find the good old U.S. of A. ...

No, the fact is, America really is crazy when it comes to drugs. I mean, don't forget, we're the ones who thought that we could prohibit alcohol. So think about our global drug war, not as any sort of rational policy, but as the international projection of a domestic psychosis. ...

There's probably never been a drug-free society. Virtually every society has ingested psychoactive substances to deal with pain, increase our energy, socialize, even commune with God. ...

So, our true challenge is to learn how to live with drugs, so they cause the least possible harm and in some cases the greatest possible benefit.

I'll tell you something else I learned, that the reason some drugs are legal and others not has almost nothing to do with science, or health, or the relative risks of drugs, and almost everything to do with who uses and who is perceived to use particular drugs.

In the late 19th century, when most of the drugs that are now illegal were legal, the principal consumers of opiates in my country and others were middle-aged white women, using them to alleviate aches and pains when few other analgesics were available. And nobody thought about criminalizing it back then, because nobody wanted to put Grandma behind bars. But when hundreds of thousands of Chinese started showing up in my country, working hard on the railroads and the mines, and then kicking back in the evening just like they had in the old country with a few puffs on that opium pipe, that's when you saw the first drug prohibition laws in California and Nevada, driven by racist fears of Chinese transforming white women into opium-addicted sex slaves. The first cocaine prohibition laws were similarly prompted by racist fears of black men sniffing that white powder and forgetting their proper place in Southern society. And the first marijuana prohibition laws, all about fears of Mexican migrants in the West and the Southwest. ...

And what drives me is my shame at living in an otherwise great nation that has less than five percent of the world's population but almost 25 percent of the worlds' incarcerated population. It's the people I meet who have lost someone they love to drug-related violence, or prison or overdose or AIDS because our drug policies emphasize criminalization over health. It's good people who have lost their jobs, their homes, their freedom, even their children to the state, not because they hurt anyone, but solely because they chose to use one drug instead of another.

So, is legalization the answer? On that, I'm torn... legally regulating and taxing most of the drugs that are now criminalized would radically reduce the crime, violence, corruption and black markets, and the problems of adulterated and unregulated drugs, and improve public safety, and allow taxpayer resources to be developed to more useful purposes. ...

People tend to think of prohibition as the ultimate form of regulation when in fact it represents the abdication of regulation with criminals filling the void. ...what we really need to do is to bring the underground drug markets as much as possible aboveground and regulate them as intelligently as we can, to minimize both the harms of drugs and the harms of prohibitionist policies. ...

Look at Portugal, where nobody goes to jail for possessing drugs and the government's made a serious commitment to treating addiction as a health issue. ...

So, the challenges we face today are twofold:

The first is the policy challenge of designing and implementing alternatives to ineffective prohibitionist policies, even as we need to get better at regulating and living with the drugs that are now legal.

But the second challenge is tougher, because it's about us. The obstacles to reform lie not just out there in the power of the prison industrial complex or other vested interests that want to keep things the way they are, but within each and every one of us. It's our fears and our lack of knowledge and imagination that stands in the way of real reform.

And ultimately, I think that boils down to the kids, and to every parent's desire to put our baby in a bubble, and the fear that somehow drugs will pierce that bubble and put our young ones at risk. In fact, sometimes it seems the entire War on Drugs gets justified as one great big child protection act, which any young person can tell you it's not.

So here's what I say to teenagers:

First, don't do drugs.

Second, don't do drugs.

Third, if you do do drugs, there's some things I want you to know, because my bottom line as your parent is come home safely at the end of the night, and grow up and lead a healthy and good adulthood. That's my drug education mantra: Safety first.

So this is what I've dedicated my life to, to building an organization and a movement of people who believe we need to turn our backs on the failed prohibitions of the past and embrace new drug policies grounded in science, compassion, health, and human rights, where people who come from across the political spectrum and every other spectrum as well, where people who love our drugs, people who hate drugs, and people who don't give a damn about drugs, but every one of us believe that this War on Drugs, this backward, heartless, disastrous War on Drugs has got to end. Thank you.

Like Ethan Nadelmann's 2014 TEDTalk, the Drug Policy Alliance has played – and continues to play – an important role in my education regarding the failed war on drugs, social injustice, mass incarceration, harm reduction, and more. The Drug Policy Alliance states:

The Drug Policy Alliance is the leading organization in the United States working to end the war on drugs, repair its harms, and build a better approach. We envision a just society in which the use and regulation of drugs are grounded in science, compassion, health, and human rights. (Drug Policy Alliance, 2020, p.1)

Drug possession is the most arrested offense in the United States, with one person arrested every 23 seconds. An arrest, even if it doesn't result in a conviction, can lead to loss of employment, housing, parental rights, immigration status, and more. This overemphasis on criminalization distorts systems of care for people struggling with substance use disorders, contributing to an acute shortage of services for those who need and want them, and represents a vast waste of government resources. (Drug Policy Alliance, 2020, p.10)

The criminalization of drugs is a devastating form of systemic oppression. Black people in the U.S. are three times more likely to be arrested for drug use than white people, despite using drugs at the same rate – and in some places, the disparities are far greater. Latinx people are also disproportionately harmed by the criminal legal system, although there is a serious lack of data due to how most states report criminalization statistics. (Drug Policy Alliance, 2020, p.11)

By any measure and every metric, the U.S. war on drugs – a constellation of laws and policies that seeks to prevent and control the use and sale of drugs primarily through punishment and coercion – has been a colossal failure with tragic results. Indeed, federal and state policies that are designed to be "tough" on people who use and sell drugs have helped over-fill our jails and prisons, permanently branded millions of people as "criminals," and exacerbated drug-related death, disease and suffering – all while failing at their stated goal of reducing problematic drug use. (Drug Policy Alliance, 2017, p. 2)

Drug decriminalization is a critical next step toward achieving a rational drug policy that puts science and public health before punishment and incarceration. (Drug Policy Alliance, 2017, p. 2)

Decriminalization means that people are no longer arrested or incarcerated merely for possessing or using a drug. (Drug Policy Alliance, 2017, p. 4)

Removing criminal penalties for drug use and possession will save billions of dollars a year that can be used to provide effective health interventions for those who need them, while focusing criminal justice resources on serious public safety problems. (Drug Policy Alliance, 2017, p. 13)

Johann Hari, author of "Chasing the Scream," on Twitter February 27, 2019:

"The core of addiction is not wanting to be present in your life, because your life is too painful a place to be. This is why imposing more pain or punishment on a person with an addiction problem actually makes their addiction worse."

What really changed how I saw substance use, drug policy/drug laws, the failed drug war, addiction, and treatment was when I first learned about harm reduction. The concept of harm reduction changed everything for me. There is not one specific definition for harm reduction, so I am including several:

Drug Policy Alliance:

Harm reduction is a set of ideas and interventions that seek to reduce the harms associated with both drug use and ineffective, racialized drug policies. Harm reduction stands in stark contrast to a punitive approach to drug use. It is based on acknowledging the dignity and humanity of people who use drugs and bringing them into a community of care in order to minimize negative consequences and promote optimal health and social inclusion. We believe that every solution with the potential to promote the health and well-being of people who use drugs and to mitigate drug related harm should be considered. We seek innovative approaches to drug use, drug treatment, and drug policy based on science and research. (Drug Policy Alliance, 2021, p. 9)

Over the Influence: The Harm Reduction Guide to Controlling Your Drug and Alcohol Use:

Harm reduction is a way to help people change their substance use without demanding immediate and lifelong abstinence. It uses many creative strategies to keep people alive and safe while they figure out how to develop a healthier relationship with drugs. For some people, that means abstinence; for others that means moderate or safer use.

Harm reduction takes a health perspective, rather than a moral or legal perspective, on drug use. Drug use is not bad. It is a normal human behavior, and most people don't get in trouble because of it. Drug misuse is a habit that has gotten out of hand, or it is a signal of other co-occurring problems.

Harm reduction attends to every aspect of health – physical, mental and emotional, social, and economic. It is nonjudgmental, compassionate, and pragmatic – it starts where the person is, stays with the person through the entire process of change, and never ever kicks anyone out. (Denning & Little, 2017, p. 197)

Zachary Siegel's article "We Know How to Treat Opioid Addiction" is the article that gave me a clear understanding of methadone and buprenorphine, the gold standard medications for opioid use disorder. It's from 2016, but I saved it, planning to use it in Lizabeth's book, because I believe strongly that it has the power to change people's minds and perspectives. As it did mine. Portions of Zachary Siegel's "We Know How to Treat Opioid Addiction," published online in Slate, *on November 30, 2016 follow:*

Fortunately, we have a proven way of lowering the death rate and easing the ills of addiction: medication-assisted treatments like methadone and buprenorphine. Unfortunately, thanks to a moral and policy-driven opposition to these treatment techniques, we're not using it.

The first hurdle comes from misunderstanding how medication-assisted treatment works. Here's the science behind it: Our brain produces natural opioids. But with the continued flooding of external opioids like heroin, the brain gradually stops producing its own. An internally depleted opioid system leaves us constantly sore, sensitive to pain, depressed, fatigued but unable to sleep. When I was still addicted but not using, I always felt a pang of doom impossible to relieve. These medications – which are synthetic and semi-synthetic opioids – help stabilize users and staunch these side effects while giving the brain a chance to heal.

Once maintained on the right dose, the receptor sites are activated just enough to keep the opioid system sated without producing the intense highs and lows (the hallmark of addiction) of opioids like heroin. This gives the brain, and most importantly, one's connection with the world, a chance to rebuild. Simply put, these medications hydrate a thirsty system. On these drugs we can work, drive, and behave virtually indistinguishably from ordinary Janes and Joes.

The World Health Organization calls these medications **"essential"** because expanding access to them reduces crime, infectious disease, and death. In blocking access, these all rise.

Given all of this, it should come as a shock that only a **quarter** of patients who sought treatment for opioid-use disorders in the U.S. received these medications. This is particularly problematic because drug treatment programs have a notoriously high dropout rate. Those that are given these medications stay engaged in the process for longer than those who don't use them.

Outside of the lab, certain areas provide a real-world testament to the medications' effectiveness: In 1995, during an HIV outbreak in France, the government instituted what's called a "low threshold model" that let doctors prescribe methadone and buprenorphine on demand. Since 2004, France has seen a remarkable **80 percent reduction** in overdose deaths.

America needs to implement this model. But there is rampant misinformation, rigid ideological resistance, and outdated policy that keeps it from happening. To prescribe opioids to a person addicted to them simply does not compute with America's deeply carved grooves of a medication-adverse, 12-step self-help culture that dominates our version of addiction treatment. Close to 80 percent of our residential treatment centers are steeped in the 12 steps of Alcoholics Anonymous, many of which operate on unscientific beliefs about which medications are appropriate.

I often hear medication-assisted treatment called "trading one addiction for another." This stems from a fundamental misunderstanding of what addiction is. Addiction, as defined by psychiatry, is the agonizing, compulsive pursuit of a behavior despite the negative consequences said behavior reaps. The perturbed opioid system that users experience – the thing that makes it so hard for them to actively live in the world – is a medical problem. Why wouldn't we use a medication to treat it?

My friend Hal kindly volunteered his experience to illustrate why he's not addicted to buprenorphine, which he has taken for a couple years. He's 26 and had a brutal habit that occupied his formative years. After a near-death overdose, a detox facility gave him the drug and referred him to a doctor to prescribe it. Now, he takes this maintenance drug, lives with his sister in Chicago, works as a barber, and contributes to his community.

So where is the addiction? He's no longer stealing his grandmother's jewelry to buy drugs. Hal left his addiction behind when he rejoined the world with the help of buprenorphine. Hal would go into withdrawal without the drug, but that is not addiction. That is what's called physical dependence, and it happens to anybody and everybody who takes opioids. His vocation, his relationships, that he thinks life is worth living, is excited about what the future holds – this is what recovery looks like. It doesn't matter what molecules are in his bloodstream.

Nonetheless, a collective miasma emanating from a treatment industry deems Hal as not being truly in recovery because he's still taking some form of opioid. Frustratingly, it took Hal three different treatment attempts that cost his family tens of thousands of dollars before he finally found the doctor who gave him buprenorphine. And that doctor was not affiliated with any residential treatment facility (an industry that rakes in an estimated $35 billion per year).

The stigma against these medications also comes in the form of policy barriers. For no other drug does a doctor need to take an eight-hour course, get licensed by the DEA, and adhere to strict patient limits, but these strict standards reduce the number of doctors even able to prescribe methadone and buprenorphine. ...

The recovery community and treatment staff at treatment centers have a long way to go, both in terms of use and perception. Someone with diabetes who takes insulin and receives nutritional counseling is simply receiving "treatment." Not insulin-assisted treatment or counseling-assisted treatment. So why do we still refer to methadone or buprenorphine use as medication-assisted treatment? It's time to drop the "assisted" modifier here – medication for opioid users is simply treatment. Perhaps if we can do that, more widespread acceptance of a treatment method that can save lives will follow. (Siegel, 2016)

Maia Szalavitz gives her "prescription" for how to improve treatment for addiction. "Deep Systemic Change: My 10 Steps to Transform Addiction Treatment," published in Filter *magazine on October 8, 2018. Portions follow:*

I'd like to lay out the rudiments of what would actually help – and which measures matter most.

1.   Genuinely expand access to medication treatment – yesterday. We have two drugs that are proven to cut the death rate from opioid addiction by half or more when used long term: methadone and buprenorphine. Anyone who is addicted to opioids and wants to get even a single dose once should be able to access these medications on demand – in hospitals, doctor's offices, emergency rooms and syringe exchange programs. Minimal restrictions, for example, to prevent people from getting more than one dose per day, may be justified – but that's it. No urines or counseling or abstinence from opioids or other substances should be required to get these drugs, just as those barriers are not imposed on people with other disorders who need medication.

2.   Stop forced tapering of pain patients and provide real access to proven alternatives.

No evidence shows benefit from forced taper; some suggests severe harm. The only realistic way to reduce reliance on opioids for chronic pain – which is still necessary for some patients and will continue to be in the foreseeable future – is to provide effective alternatives.

3.   Create a tiered system for addiction medication access. There are three primary uses of medication treatment: harm reduction, stabilization and ongoing care. Consequently, we need three separate tracks of programming to meet each of these specific needs. For harm reduction, what's needed is a welcoming place where people can simply get a dose of medication and see some friendly faces. For stabilization, people who want to put their lives back together need easy access to services that meet their particular needs… After people have been stabilized, however, they will need the third track…This track – sometimes called "medical maintenance" – basically requires a once-a-month

check-in to get medication via a primary care doctor and ensure all is well.

4. End insurance coverage, Medicaid or other government funding for rehabs and "sober homes" that reject the use of medication; provide no coverage of 12-step focused content. And there remains no sensible reason why insurers and governments should pay for self-help people can already get for free, instead of funding effective alternatives (such as cognitive behavioral therapy or motivational enhancement therapy) that do not raise issues related to moral judgment ("character defects") or the First Amendment.

5. Create and fund a full range of harm reduction services. In order to save lives, we need safer consumption spaces in areas where drug use and sales are concentrated; syringe exchange programs scaled to meet demand; and increased access to supplies like fentanyl-checking test strips. We also need shelters and housing, separate from those aimed at stabilization and abstinence, for people who are actively addicted, many of whom are also mentally ill and have symptoms related to severe trauma. When people have safe places to live and to use drugs, they are both much more likely to survive and much more likely to find ways to sustained recovery.

6. Decouple "beds" from treatment. People with addiction have a wide range of individual needs and institutional "programs" will never be able to meet all of them. "Sober homes" also tend to be based on a 12-step ideology, which is fine for those who find that pathway amenable, but not for those who don't – and not when that ideology is interpreted to stigmatize and discourage medication use. For most illnesses, medical and psychiatric, people recover better when they can stay in their own home with their family and friends nearby. This can be more complicated in addiction if friends and

family are not supportive of recovery, or are actively addicted themselves. But many people with addiction are not in that situation and all will eventually need to manage cues and other sources of stress in the community where they live. Consequently, "beds" are only really needed for people who are either homeless, living in an unsafe situation or psychiatrically or medically complicated enough to require inpatient medication stabilization. This is not the majority of people with addiction, even with opioid addiction. The mental health field has recognized that institutionalization is generally harmful and that when needed, should only be used for the shortest possible time. Addiction treatment needs to catch up. We need a system that provides a menu of individualized options – not residences staffed mainly by non-medical people that charge inpatient hospital care rates.

7. Create an FDA-like system to approve – or reject – psychological and addiction treatments. For all the problems with psychiatric drugs and their regulation, at least before they are sold they are required to be proven effective with minimal harm – and if harms are later discovered, they can be pulled from the market. The same is not true for talk therapies: Anyone can claim anything is effective and it's extremely hard to "recall" harmful approaches – like the confrontation and humiliation that are still used in some addiction and teen programs.

8. Recognize the implications of poly drug use. Around half of all addictions – and a similar proportion of overdoses – involve multiple drugs. Addiction is not caused by any particular drug. It is caused by people discovering that altering their consciousness in certain ways helps them cope in particular environments – and then continuing to do so after it has become more harmful than helpful. Typically, the most traumatized

and severely mentally ill people use many different drugs in many combinations – and when someone's goal is to obliterate, rather than alter, their consciousness, reducing risk can be challenging. All services aimed at people with addiction need to consider the needs of poly drug users, while also recognizing that for some, one drug is problematic while another can be managed successfully or even used to reduce harm (e.g., marijuana instead of or in order to reduce opioids).

9. Decriminalize drug possession. ... The primary purpose of criminalization is to stigmatize drug use and people who take drugs – if criminalization is to deter people, it must stigmatize. And that stigma, of course, is a huge barrier to getting people into treatment whether for addiction or for overdose; to making treatment more effective; to expanding harm reduction; and basically to everything we need to do to end the crisis. Criminalization also makes services less user-friendly because so many people are coerced into treatment by legal sanctions. Ending this practice, or at least reducing it, would force providers to do more to attract patients – and the more compassionate and welcoming addiction treatment is, the more effective it is.

10. Make universal healthcare happen. If we really want to fight addiction in the long run, safe, evidence-based care must be available to everyone who needs it. (Szalavitz, 2018)

In November 2020, Oregon decriminalized all drugs. Zachary Siegel reports on this landmark happening in The Baffler *article, online, "The Oregon Model" on November 17, 2020. Portions follow:*

Until recently, the good guys have been perennial losers in a country of unyielding criminalization, mass incarceration, and D.A.R.E. officers peddling propaganda to grade schoolers.

The morning after election night [11/3/2020], though, the longtime drug policy activist [Doug McVay] woke up feeling like decades of work were not in vain: Measure 110, Oregon's ballot initiative to decriminalize the possession of small amounts of all drugs – including meth, heroin, and cocaine – and redirect funds towards substance use treatment decisively passed 58.5 to 41.5 percent.

Oregon's vote to decriminalize all drugs, making it the first in the nation to do so, marks a historic turning point in that struggle. "Oregon showed the world that a more humane, compassionate approach is possible," said Kassandra Frederique, executive director of the Drug Policy Alliance, a nonprofit advocacy group that spent millions backing Measure 110...

During the 1990s, Portugal's drug problems looked a lot like America's do now: opioid overdoses were rampant, and at one point, the country had the highest HIV transmission rate in the European Union. Portugal's drug laws were likewise harsh, with roughly half of people in prison there for drug-related offenses. The American way – criminalize, criminalize, criminalize – utterly failed to bring results in Portugal, so they ran in the opposite direction. In 2001, Portugal became the first country in the world to decriminalize all drugs and invest heavily in treatment and social services. The country has made remarkable progress in the years since, and what became known as the "Portugal Model" is celebrated by activists around the world.

What's happening in Oregon is "the Portugal model on a state level," McVay said. "We've seen it work successfully in another country for twenty years. Treating people who use drugs as others, stigmatized and brutalized, is what causes the real drug problems. We're getting people to understand that."

There's an important lesson for Americans to take away from Portugal's story: decriminalization was only the first step. Shifting the culture is what ultimately transformed the country and led to the drop in incarceration and addiction rates. Instead of being considered criminals and junkies, people struggling with drug use and addiction began to finally be treated with dignity and respect. You cannot humanize people you deem to be criminal. (Siegel, 2020)

Elizabeth spent the last three years of her life in Palm Beach County, Florida. At that time, there were no legal syringe exchanges in the state of Florida. Elizabeth cleaned her needles with bleach. Rebel Recovery Florida now runs the second syringe exchange in Florida, in Palm Beach County. Portions of "In a Florida 'Recovery' Hub, a Syringe Program Finds Its Place" by Umme Hoque in Filter *magazine on May 20, 2021 follow:*

Organizers at Rebel Recovery Florida say their slogan is simple: "We love you."

As of April 1, Rebel Recovery Florida runs only the second SSP [Syringe Services Program] in South Florida, following the successful launch of a pilot in Miami-Dade County [IDEA] in December 2016. But the harm reduction nonprofit has been showing up for people in Palm Beach County for over five years, starting with Kunzelman informally providing friends with syringes when they needed them. Following 2019's legalization of SSP in Florida, Palm Beach County became the second in the state to approve such a program.

The Rebel Recovery philosophy is that anyone who wants to seek support for drug use, not just those who want to stop their use, is in recovery. "We're merging these worlds that everyone sees as opposite – harm reduction and recovery," Kunzelman said. "To us, they're the same thing."

As the overdose crisis takes more and more lives across the country, and HIV outbreaks spread as community SSP [Syringe Services Programs] are under fire, programs like Rebel Recovery could mean the difference between life and death for locals who use drugs. Recent studies also found that hospitals across Florida could save millions of dollars if SSP were more prevalent.

Kunzelman and his team aim to support 200 participants this year. Per state law, they can only provide syringes on a 1:1 exchange basis, meaning that participants have to bring in used syringes in order to receive new ones. Participants can register through an anonymous system that allows them to legally carry unused syringes. The agency also offers HIV screenings, community-based support groups, recovery services and a recovery community center, healthcare services, weekly food distribution, outreach, online support groups and workshops.

For Kunzelman, these tools empower people. "We provide the knowledge they need to take charge of their own health. We're not 'abstinence-first'… or 'drug-free.'"

The abstinence model is pervasive in Palm Beach County. The county houses some of the largest rehab facilities in the country, most of which are "abstinence-first or-only" and require health insurance.

For people with Medicare, Medicaid or no insurance, or for those seeking harm reduction, finding services is challenging. Kunzelman and Nancy McConnell founded Rebel Recovery because of their own lived experience of struggling to navigate the system.

Lived experience and connection to the community are key for how Rebel Recovery operates. The majority of the agency's work is through peer services, providing education, advocacy and support for those who need it. (Hoque, 2020)

In November 2021, New York State was the first state in the United States to open safe consumption spaces or overdose present prevention centers. "Safe Consumption Sites Are Opening in New York City" by Alex Norcia in Filter *magazine on November 30, 2021 details this long awaited important victory:*

On November 30, [2021], New York City authorized two safe consumption sites to begin operations as soon as possible. The decision, a hard-fought victory for harm reduction advocates, makes them the first government-sanctioned overdose prevention centers, as they are also known, to open in the United States.

A pair of nonprofits – New York Harm Reduction Educators (NYHRE) and the Washington Heights Corner Project – are merging to create a new organization, OnePointNYC, which will operate the sites in East Harlem and Washington Heights. There, people will be able to obtain sterile syringes and other safer-use supplies, access treatment options and other services, and bring their own drugs to use, with trained staff and naloxone on hand.

In the national context, New York City's move arrives as overdose deaths have hit record highs during the coronavirus pandemic. Recent data showed that more than 100,000 people in the United States died during a 12-month period between April 2020 and April 2021, amid an increasingly adulterated illicit drug supply.

"This is a watershed milestone in the fight to end overdose deaths in New York," Melissa Moore, the director of civil systems reform at the Drug Policy Alliance, who previously led the DPA's work in the state, said in a statement. "If we want to save lives, reduce criminalization, and curb racial disparities, we need comprehensive, innovative, and forward-thinking approaches like Overdose Prevention Centers."

As DPA notes, approximately 120 sanctioned SCS already operate in 10 countries around the world, and "over 100 evidence-based, peer-reviewed studies have consistently proven the positive impacts of supervised consumption services." The organization lists some of these demonstrated benefits as follows:

Increasing entry into substance use disorder treatment
Reducing the amount and frequency that clients use drugs
Reducing public disorder and public injecting while increasing public safety
Reducing HIV and Hepatitis C risk behavior (i.e. syringe sharing, unsafe sex)
Successfully managing frequent on-site overdoses and reducing drug-related overdose death rates (there has not been a single overdose fatality at any SCS worldwide)
Saving costs due to reduction in disease, overdose deaths, and need for emergency medical services
Increasing the delivery of medical and social services (Norcia, 2021)

I want to point out that Elizabeth's drug use was from 2004 to 2014. Drug use has become much more dangerous since her time. Elizabeth's drug use was before fentanyl, before the beginning of the overdose crisis. Now we have fentanyl in the drug supply, and we went through the

250

Covid-19 pandemic. Additionally, xylazine, known as "tranq," a horse tranquilizer not meant for humans, is on the scene. Elizabeth's story and this Epilogue were largely written before fentanyl, the overdose crisis, Covid, and xylazine. Articles from harm reduction sources like *Filter* magazine (https://filtermag.org) discuss what steps can be taken to reduce the harm and save the lives of people who use drugs.

Concluding Thoughts

I believe that if Elizabeth and I had been aware of and had understood harm reduction, MAT (Medication Assisted Treatment), syringe exchanges, overdose prevention centers...her life might have been happier and healthier – and she might have lived longer. Elizabeth might have continued using substances, but the support of a harm reduction community certainly could have improved her quality of life. I believe if Elizabeth had come to the point where she wanted to stop or moderate her substance use, first she would have needed to find safe shelter – with safe sleeping, access to food, water, medical care, mental health counseling – NOT contingent upon her being free of substances. Elizabeth would have needed assistance, perhaps from a harm reduction program, to find this type of housing – that might have made it possible for her to attempt positive change.

Instead of harm reduction, Elizabeth got incarceration.

Elizabeth was caught up in the criminal legal system when she was just 19 years old. She had never been in trouble, had no juvenile record. Elizabeth ended up being sentenced to three years in state prison. New Jersey's "Truth in Sentencing" told us that meant probably nine months in state prison. She had already served six months in jail, so Elizabeth would probably only serve three months in state prison. But Elizabeth's parole was violated twice due to positive drug tests, so she spent much more time in state prison than was expected.

253

Jails and prisons are actively harmful. Prisons are a breeding ground for racial discord, violence, indignity, harassment, bullying... It goes without saying that Elizabeth did not get the help she needed in the more than three years she spent in jails and state prison. Prison, where inmates are treated "like the scum of the earth," – as Elizabeth told me in her letters – just made her life much worse. Losing her connections to her family, her friends, and being separated from her son worsened her mental health issues and made future drug use very likely to be MORE chaotic. In addition, when Elizabeth left prison, she couldn't get any type of assistance from the state – housing assistance, for example – because she had drug charges. When Elizabeth was released from prison and tried to find work, her felony drug charges made her job search difficult and her options limited. Elizabeth never should have gone to jail or prison. No one should be incarcerated for possessing or using a substance.

Elizabeth attended six 12-step rehabs (her second 12-step rehab was court-ordered and locked).

When Elizabeth entered her fifth 12-step rehab in less than four years, just six weeks earlier her husband had taken her six-month-old baby from her arms and put her on a plane "home." Besides desperately missing her baby, Elizabeth had issues:

1. Threat of prison for several drug possession charges
2. Poly substance addiction – heroin, crack, weed, alcohol, – as well as sex addiction
3. Diagnoses of depression, an eating disorder, generalized anxiety disorder, PTSD, post-partum depression, self-harm
4. Childhood sexual abuse

Here are Elizabeth's notes from a lecture, in her fifth 12-step rehab, after almost three weeks of "treatment":

Guaranteed Sobriety (July 17, 2008)

1) Pray in the morning – ask God to keep me clean, ask for help
2) Go to a meeting, get phone #'s, Step or Big Book Meeting
3) Read something spiritual, inspirational
4) Talk to another addict, preferably @ the sponsor level
5) Pray @ night, thank God for keeping me clean & sober that day

Elizabeth believed in God. I believe in God. I am happy for ANY way a person can recover. I have friends who have been supported by participation in AA/NA. But that is the point – the 12-steps are support, not treatment. The above "Guaranteed Sobriety" note, written during one of the rehab's lectures, is simply not evidence-based treatment. I wish Elizabeth and I had understood that she needed effective treatment for her issues, and she needed to learn new coping skills – skills to replace the substances and behaviors that were her main coping mechanisms. An individual's specific needs/issues are not adequately addressed in abstinence based 12-step inpatient rehabs.

On **March 13, 2009**, while in jail, Elizabeth wrote, "I think my addiction is a result of a genetic predisposition & my perception of how I was treated, my lack of self-esteem/self-confidence, & the shame of sexual abuse."

Elizabeth had some insight. But as illustrated by the above "Guaranteed Sobriety" rehab notes, the 12-step rehabs Elizabeth attended focused on 12-step principles and on abstinence. An individual's needs and issues were less important than the 12 steps and the goal of abstinence. Aftercare was always "90 [AA/NA] meetings in 90 days." Elizabeth's experience of not being helped by multiple stints in 12-step rehabs is unfortunately quite common.

255

That's why we often hear of people going to rehab five, ten, or even many more times. Matthew Perry, one of the stars of the hit TV show "Friends," went to rehab 15 times (Perry, 2022, p. 46). Elizabeth did NOT fail treatment. "Treatment" failed Elizabeth.

Elizabeth lived almost six years after losing her son Riley. She told me she saw no reason not to get high after her husband took her baby from her arms. 12-step rehabs were never going to help Elizabeth because their message was: "Stop using all substances forever." 12-step rehabs didn't attempt to reconnect her with her son, work through the pain of losing him, or treat her mental illness and trauma. Only the court-ordered locked rehab put her on medication in an attempt to treat her diagnosed mental illness. Even jails and prison put her on medication for her depression and anxiety. The coping skills 12-step rehabs imparted were just directives to work the steps, get a sponsor, read the AA big book, and go to meetings. It is simply illogical to think these 12-step rehabs are enough to "fix" people who are dealing with mental illness and/or trauma.

Elizabeth got kicked out of two or three rehabs for fraternization. There are 12-step meetings for sex/love addiction – a behavioral addiction that the 12-step movement recognizes. The six rehabs Elizabeth attended all failed to address or treat her sex addiction – which she was honest about. I do not believe rehabs should admit every single prospective paying client. If a rehab doesn't actively treat sex addiction, they should not take clients who say sex addiction is an issue. If a rehab doesn't have a psychiatrist on staff prepared to prescribe medication, they should not admit people with serious mental health issues. A rehab should not admit a person with trauma, PTSD, sexual abuse issues... if they do not have therapists specifically qualified to work with trauma issues.

I agree with Maia Szalavitz (2018) when she says only the most medically severe cases or those in a dangerous living situation need inpatient rehab. Intensive outpatient, often known as IOP, makes more sense. Inpatient rehab is a break from real life. You have a bed, a shower, and food provided to you. You are constantly with a group of people who all are experiencing negative consequences related to their addiction(s). Connections form easily. For people whose problems are serious enough to enter rehab, it feels really good to make friends who understand. But when you leave rehab, those intense rehab friendships usually disappear. You are back to being responsible for your own shelter, food, etc. Your loved ones expect a lot from you. Many times, you are right back in the environment where your issues started and/or became problematic. You haven't learned new coping skills because you didn't get evidence-based treatment – you mostly just learned 12-step stuff.

Relapse after leaving rehab is common – and dangerous for people with an opioid use disorder, who have lost their tolerance. The same lowered tolerance and overdose risk applies to people with an opioid use disorder when they leave jail or prison. It would make sense if every person with an opioid use disorder who leaves rehab, jail, or prison were given naloxone to take with them.

Naloxone is the medication that reverses opioid overdoses. The brand name of naloxone is Narcan. When a person uses opioids, the opioids slow down the central nervous system, which can cause slowed/stopped breathing and can lead to death. Naloxone blocks the effects of opioids on the brain and restores breathing. Saving lives. Naloxone only works on a person with opioids in their system. If naloxone is given to a person with no opioids in their system, it does not harm them. A person cannot get high from using naloxone.

People with an opioid use disorder who get treatment with methadone or buprenorphine reduce their risk of overdose. An article by Sasha Walek published February 25, 2020 on the NYU Langone website described a collaborative study between researchers at NYU Grossman School of Medicine, Johns Hopkins Bloomberg School of Public Health, the Maryland Department of Health, and multiple Maryland state agencies. The study found that "People with an opioid use disorder (OUD) receiving treatment with opioid agonists (medications such as methadone or buprenorphine) had an 80 percent lower risk of dying from an opioid overdose compared with people in treatment without the use of medications."

I am very happy to share that Elizabeth's soul mate, Matt, after a number of unsuccessful 12-step rehabs, found MAT (Medication Assisted Treatment) for his opioid use disorder. I sent Matt an early edition of Elizabeth's book.

Email from Matt, August 23, 2019

Sheila,

I just finished reading this [Elizabeth's book] in its entirety. To be honest, I just want to put my fist through the wall. Liz deserved so much better. She is the most beautiful person I have ever met and got eaten alive and treated like garbage by friends, men, and a corrupt system of "recovery" programs that have absolutely no idea how to treat addicts with addictions stronger than most peoples'. I've been married for five years, have a great job, and freedom from that insatiable urge to use that, for people like Liz and me, can't be taken away by reading the big book and asking God to remove the cravings. …

Being kicked out of whatever bullshit halfway house I happened to be at, and being told that if I had just worked "the program" correctly I wouldn't be in that situation. I know Liz probably experienced something similar, thinking the problem was her. Why did I deserve to find MAT

258

[Medicated Assisted Treatment]? Why couldn't she have discovered it? I want her back so bad, it breaks my heart. Liz and I were never high together and that means a lot to me. What we had together was the most beautiful thing I have ever experienced. What we had was not just physical, but a connection on such a deep emotional level that words cannot describe. I will never stop loving her...

Poems by Liz

Lizzie _____, where have you been?
shooting dope & wondering when
this hell will end
you'll find your friend
your true love Matt
he's the only one
besides your mom & son
who can take away the pain
or fix your fucked up brain

Mommy, I'm sorry
for screwing up entirely
when we both thought
that I'd had all I'd want
I don't think I can promise anymore
but until I walk out these doors
I'll do my best to walk the line
and like Cassiopeia I'll shine

I'll get no sterling accolades
what used to be shining now fades
am I a lost kind of soul?
or can I be made whole?

should I go or should I stay
fuck that...
I will cry away my tears
and try to forget these years
that weigh upon my soul
how did I get so old?

How many hearts has she broken?
how many dreams has she stolen?
leaving death and destruction
will he be the next one?
a trail of blood & tears
kidding herself it will last for years
she's the kinda girl inspiring glory
but she's guaranteed to leave you in fury

her hair's spun gold
I don't have to be told
there's more to this woman
than meets the eye
we're one & the same
again we meet
by chance
some fucked up
kind of sisterhood
of travelling, junkie pants
we've shared secrets
we've shared moments
cried together
lied together
could have died together

I am a succubus

and if you must
take off in the night
I might not put up a fight
I'll swallow up your soul
whether it's tattered or whole
I'll just walk out your door
stealing all I can and more

I'll make your whole world fall apart
if Cupid misses his mark
I'll be left alone naked: stark
solitary in the dark
surrounded by demons
a soul ravaged by cretins

saving grace or saving face
can't these years just be erased?
spoiled milk & spoiled dreams
instead of pages, I've got reams

made 1000's more mistakes
all at the week's break
thought I could handle this
now at myself I shake my fist

with this disease I am afflicted
and my soul it's been convicted
my very being's addicted
yet my heart it is conflicted

References

Denning, P., & Little J. (2017). *Over the influence: The harm reduction guide to controlling your drug and alcohol use* (2nd ed.). The Guilford Press.

Drug Policy Alliance. (2017). *It's time for the U.S. to decriminalize drug use and possession.* https://web.archive.org/web/20210417230824/https://drugpolicy.org/sites/default/files/documents/Drug_Policy_Alliance_Time_to_Decriminalize_Report_July_2017.pdf

Drug Policy Alliance. (2020). *We were built for this moment: Drug Policy Alliance 2020 annual report.* https://web.archive.org/web/20210417180937/https://drugpolicy.org/sites/default/files/dpa-2020-annual-report.pdf

Drug Policy Alliance. (2021). *The Drug Policy Alliance 2021 roadmap.* https://web.archive.org/web/20221207090031/https://drugpolicy.org/sites/default/files/2021.02.25_2021_transition_doc_0.pdf

Hoque, U. (2021, May 20). In a Florida "recovery" hub, a syringe program finds its place. *Filter.* https://filtermag.org/florida-harm-reduction-recovery/

Norcia, A. (2021, November 30). Safe consumption sites are opening in New York City. *Filter.* https://filtermag.org/safe-consumption-new-york-city/

Perry, M. (2022). *Friends, lovers, and the big terrible thing.* Flatiron Books.

Siegel, Z. (2020, November 17). The Oregon model. *The Baffler.* https://thebaffler.com/latest/the-oregon-model-siegel

Siegel, Z. (2016, November 30). We know how to treat opioid addiction. *Slate.* https://slate.com/technology/2016/11/we-do-not-use-an-evidence-backed-method-for-treating-heroin-addiction.html

Szalavitz, M. (2018, October 8). Deep systemic change: My 10 steps to transform addiction treatment. *Filter.* https://filtermag.org/transforming-addiction-treatment-my-10-steps-to-deep-systemic-change/

TED. (2014, November 12). *Why we need to end the war on drugs* [Video]. YouTube. https://www.youtube.com/watch?v=uWfLwKH_Eko

Walek, S. (2020, February 25). Medication treatments led to 80 percent lower risk of fatal overdose for patients with opioid use disorder. *NYU Langone.* https://nyulangone.org/news/medication-treatments-led-80-percent-lower-risk-fatal-overdose-patients-opioid-use-disorder

Made in United States
North Haven, CT
23 October 2023